Why People Don't Do Their Jobs

Why People Don't Do Their Jobs

The Four Root Causes of Everything

JAMES A. SHELL

Other Disclaimer: The content of this book is for entertainment purposes only. It is given in good faith based on my experience as an auditor and quality systems professional. You, the user, are accepting the risk of errors and omissions, bad decisions and implementation issues.

Hiring me as a consultant to help you do these activities is not for entertainment purposes, please contact me for more information.

Contents

Why People Don't Do Their Jobs

01 Introduction

Your flight is canceled, your electric blender has been recalled, you can't make a doctor's appointment without literally sitting next to the phone hoping they'll call you back.

Your cheap toys break as you get them out of the package. You can't get a straight answer from customer service. The Help Desk is helpless.

You're stuck in traffic in a junky car in which the heater doesn't work. Your smartphone isn't very smart. The list gets longer.

Every day there is news of some mass disaster that is entirely preventable. The institutions that were put up to prevent it are breaking down.

Sorry to be such a downer. All these things happen because people don't do their jobs. For some of us, who derive a revenue source from human failure, it is a golden age.

Who am I to be Writing This?

A million companies worldwide have subscribed to an international quality system standard, and I am the most customer-facing member of this system, the auditor.

I've been given unusual access to the business systems of some of the major corporations in the country, and a lot of them that aren't so major

My job is to go into these places and decide of how their quality systems are functioning. I do about 50 of these audits a year, in all sorts of environments. I've been to whiskey distillers, the dynamite factory, and several places that make cardboard and bubble wrap. I've been to the place where a crew of workers personalizes the information on your credit card (that magnetic stripe) along with the chip. I've seen concrete outhouses and railroad locomotives fly through the air on giant cranes. I've got some stories to tell.

I do a lot of work with people who are recruiters for what is now called "civilian contracting" who are the people that keep the US Military's systems safe from cyberattack, and replace their military laptop when someone drives over it with a Hummer.

A typical type of audit is a startup situation. These are people that want to live out the American Dream by inventing some sort of gadget or service that over a period gains market acceptance. They need some sort of international recognition to help their credibility.

Sometimes it doesn't work. I've seen a couple of these go the other way.

I also audit a lot of family businesses. They have a certain character of their own, and later you'll get my nuanced point of view of this type of organization.

Business Improvements
As part of this International Standard, there is a requirement to document something called a "corrective action." That's where there is some kind of screw-up, and some responsible party is required to do an investigation. It is similar enough to the investigation that happens when a plane crashes.

In each audit I go through maybe five of these. So, over the last decade I've seen evidence of something on the order of 2500 instances of human failure.

I am exposed to a seemingly endless stream of failure. It is a bit bleak, frankly.

But over the course of it all, I've determined that they fall into patterns. I am not the first one who has noticed this.

Also, as part of the investigation, the client usually does some soul searching, and analyzes the cause of the failure. A very typical method for this is called the "Five Why" analysis, which originated with the founder of Toyota in the 1930's. It basically says, in five-year-old fashion, when you have a problem, continue to ask "why" until you get to something that is actionable. I have a graphic of this below:

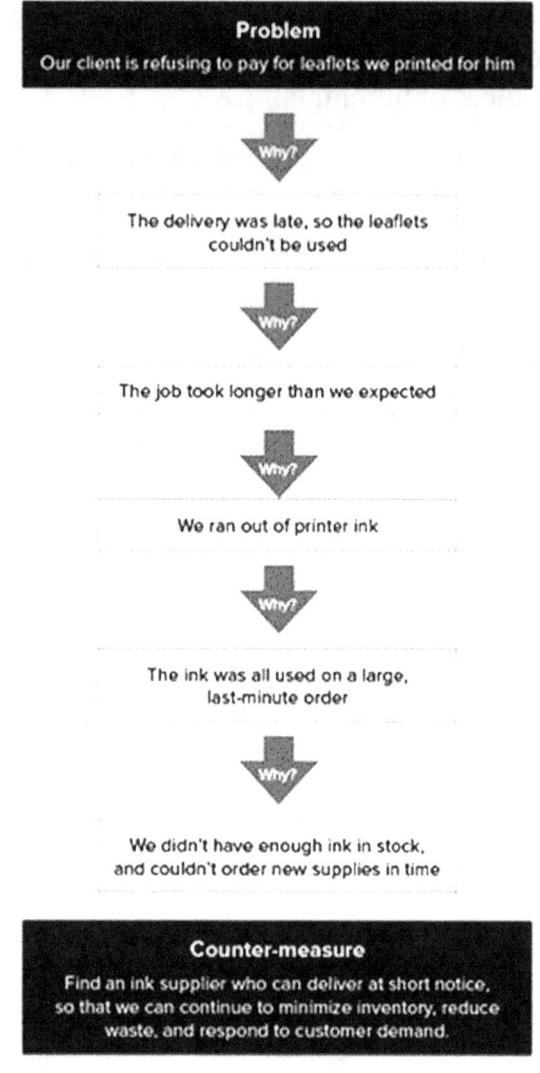

In the above example, you have a case where the company has decided on a process change, in which a better supplier is selected.

But the next question is even more interesting. Why in the hell didn't the "manager of the "purchasing process" pick up on this? The answer is that the purchasing person, if there is one, didn't do their job.

It's part of the "Toyoda" philosophy not to blame any individual employee and for the most part I agree with that. But sometimes it really is the employee's fault.

So, the next "why" in the sequence is, "why didn't the Purchasing Person do their job?" Now you get it. It asks the next question. It also opens up a can of worms.

Not asking the Last Question

90% of the 2500 of these I have seen don't ask the "next question." **Why did that person not do his or her job?**

Now it might be, in this case, that the person is perfectly innocent. There may be no way for the buyer to know how much ink usage is. In which case, the problem is the alarm or feedback system. It might be that the storage area for ink is too small, and the buyer was told at one point not to over-order. There could be a dozen reasons for this problem that are easily fixable.

Or it might be that the purchasing person didn't do their job. Or maybe the supplier didn't do their job. Investigation will tell. If there is a recurrence of the problem after the "fix" is implemented, then we'll know.

And, if we find out that the buyer didn't do their job, again, then what? Can any amount of training or retraining fix the problem? At what point do you find a better buyer? What if the buyer is the Boss's niece?

The Four Root Causes of Everything

These investigations tend to fall into patterns, like I was saying above, and the "root causes" tend to fall into one of four categories.

Category	Failure Mode
Human	Employees are impaired, disengaged, angry, unprepared to enter the workforce or simply disobedient
Procedure or Process	The process itself is screwed up to the extent that it exists. Methods, and the documents that describe them, are flawed.
Resources/Infrastructure	Resources, including equipment, IT systems, environment, or facilities are inadequate or poorly maintained.
Controls	Alarm systems and other control systems are nonexistent, don't give feedback properly, or are ignored

At the high level, at some point in the day there is also a management function that is supposed to be running the system.

A further theme of this book is the tendency for these failures to keep happening, even if management knows about it.

Some companies are mediocre, and committed to staying that way.

The Fundamental Relationship

At various points in this work I am exploring some issues with the fundamental relationship between employers and employees.

By that I mean since the dawn of history, people have entered into working relationships. Someone needs some service to be done, and someone else has some spare time and ability with which to do it.

This relationship can be very intimate, as in the case with a dentist or massage therapist, or it can be very impersonal, such as a case where someone is working in a highly repetitive task on an assembly line.

The amount of power in the relationship between employer and employee has shifted over the generations. It also is heavily dependent on what the task is, and the degree to which someone else's labor can be substituted.

We're now at a point in history where this relationship has broken down a bit, I would have to say. A lot of the dysfunction we are seeing as consumers is because of this fundamental breakdown in the capitalistic system.

This has been known to happen to the extreme every few generations.

We can spend some time later on this issue, but for the time being we're making the assumption that the world is still functioning and going to function in the way that it has for the last few decades.

Who Should Read This Book?

No, this is not children's reading. Toward the middle there are actual stories of large-scale failures that were caused by people not doing their jobs. Like all books of this type, it's a reflection of what is going on in society at this brief moment of time. I hope the future people who find this in the ruins of our burned-out buildings to be a bit of a message in a bottle.

I wrote this for you and your friends, who are sitting around at lunchtime in a restaurant waiting for your meal to be served. Your surly, disengaged server plops an underwhelming, mediocre lunch in front of you after a 90-minute wait. Why did that happen?

My message is that the server is the result of and a participant in a complex sequence of events, potentially with many layers of people not doing their jobs.

So, the reader of this book is anybody who is annoyed or afraid that at this point in history, with all of the technology and everything else, functions are breaking down. It is okay if you are afraid, this stuff has been going on for a long time.

The other reader of this book comes from something I will call a little later the "technocratic layer," which is the layer in any social organization that might have the misfortune of being in charge of any of it. It's that layer that has the only chance to fix it.

Chances are the wait person won't be reading it, unless they're studying management or something. It's not for everybody.

Further Reading

From time to time, you will encounter a link and/or QR code, and if you follow it, there is some supplemental information. A lot of these consist of a little video that I have done on this topic but may also be a link to articles and other information.

I tried hard to back some of this stuff up with some attribution. You should be able to get further background information and maybe learn how to think like a quality systems person. You can take from this a grain of salt in that "talking heads," including me, approach a problem with a certain set of biases.

Anything I don't back up is my professional opinion.

I didn't invent a lot of this, but I am trying to package this in a form that you find entertaining.

All I can do is list my qualifications and experience, which I do at the end, and let you decide whether it all makes sense.

If you make it all the way back to "about the author" you will find that I, too, am part of the technocratic layer, for what that is worth. I am not attributing any of this to any conspiracy or anyone being "evil" per se, because I don't think anyone is that well organized. I am attributing a lot of it to something that is called "entropy" which is the fundamental tendency for things to break down to its lowest form of energy.

Links and References

02 Speeding, and other forms of Disobedience

We need an example of disobedience to start with, and it is easy enough to find one. We're talking about speeding, in the car sense.

This is an easily understandable situation in which there is a set of rules, and a certain fraction of the population typically doesn't follow them. Speeding, in the car sense, is considered contraindicated from a car maintenance and safety point of view. A large amount of effort is invested in keeping you from doing it.

I suppose we are going to talk about speeding, in the drug sense, a little later. That's probably not good practice either.

Your Job as a Driver

According to the driving manual, you have two jobs as a driver: don't speed, and don't crash your car. However, as we are about to see, a lot the public speeds anyway.

Speeding as a General Practice

The source I have linked in the links and references will tell you that up to 50% of drivers admit to speeding more than 15 mph on the freeway, and 40% more than 10 mph in a residential area. This is despite the statistics showing that the chance of death in a car accident increases by 2% for every 1% increase in speed. Also, speeding is a factor in nearly ⅓ of the driving fatalities.

The police and other law enforcement entities do a lot of work to keep people from doing this, as we all know.

But does this work? Apparently not.

When a new highway is constructed, the engineers set the speed limit with the underlying expectation that 15% of the people will operate their cars unsafely. Therein is a built-in low expectation of people following standard operating procedure only 85% of the time.

Speeding as a form of Disobedience

There is a bit of divergence as it applies to peoples' attitudes toward violation of the speeding laws. Despite it breaking the law, 23% of the people think it is OK to speed on the freeway, and 14% think it is OK to speed in residential areas.

What that means is that there is a fraction of the population that knows it's wrong but does it anyway.

There are surveys of one type or another and they return a variety of lame excuses: Men are more likely to speed than women, and younger and older men are more likely to speed than the "average man."

Here are some reasons from a variety of the references on this issue:

I'm Running late.

I wasn't paying attention to the speed limit.

The speed limit is set too slow (They know better than the engineer what the correct speed should be)

It doesn't feel risky, especially in an over-engineered car (My car is immune to speed-related wrecking.)

It's fun.

I want to test/show off my fancy car/other vehicle.

Preventive Measures

There is a consistent ongoing game of cat and mouse between enforcement officials and the general public. There is general acceptance of the idea of warning people where the cops are hiding.

All of this has gone on for a long time, at least as far back as the invention of speed limits and thus, the invention of speeding.

Like a lot of other things, this may have reached its peak of social acceptance in the 1970's when one of the most famous movie stars of the day produced a lot of comedy films with speeding and/or disobedience as the main premise.

The Cannonball Run

https://youtu.be/s8BNVDUslcE?si=TK_VMQcd_tnWvk89

The cops understand that one of the ways to manage the problem is to do "deterrence" namely have cars parked alongside the road with flashing lights. People will slow down if they think there are cops around to keep them from speeding.

In the otherwise respectful nation of Japan, which is known for people doing their jobs, speeding appears to be one of the guilty pleasures. In the similarly responsible nation of Germany, where some roads are considered so well engineered that they don't have a speed limit, the attitude is a little more conservative, according to the reference.

There is innovation to help get around some of these rules, Use of radar detectors, namely gadgets that tell you that a cop is nearby measuring your speed, is legal in 48 states. If you, a quality manager in the workplace, came up on some of your employees getting out of their jobs by using some gadget, you'd be furious, if not a little impressed at their ingenuity.

Speed Cameras

A system developed a few years ago about a system of speed cameras that are affixed to speed-detecting devices. If you are found speeding, the authorities are supposedly empowered to send you a ticket in the mail.

In the US this makes people furious, so much so that these devices are banned in 8 states and can be challenged in many others. They're thought not to work. They only catch you if you are speeding, which means that you are speeding. Also, once you learn where they are, you can slow down for a bit and avoid the ticket.

There is an article in the links and references to the effect that speed cameras are considered racist. The cities supposedly set them up in areas where there is a high minority population, thus targeting enforcement in those areas.

In Australia, where these cameras are most widely accepted, it is still estimated that up to 10% of the drivers still speed. This means that it reduces the problem but does not eliminate it.

Attitude of Professional Drivers

There is a group of people whose job it is to drive. We're talking about truckers, cab drivers and the like.

Well, in the article I've linked, the attitude of truck drivers is similarly schizophrenic. 83% of these people think that speeding is unsafe, but 64% of the people do it anyway. As a side point, the people who speed more than 10 mph are 266% more likely to use a handheld phone while driving, which is well known to be just as bad as drinking. Also, these same employees are 171% more likely to do their paperwork while rolling.

A recent law was proposed to the effect that a gadget be installed in some of these trucks to keep the driver from speeding. This is being opposed by both the "trucking industry" and the drivers, presumably because it is "too boring."

The practice of speeding is so widespread that it is considered "manageable" rather than enforceable. There is an underlying expectation by cops that people are going to speed.

It appears to be common to all cultures to some extent, and gender and youth biased.

What does all of this have to do with you?

Or me, for that matter?

Assuming you're responsible for getting people to do their jobs, this is of immense importance. After having been around a bit, it has been my observation that the tendency for people to not do their jobs, like other forms of human disobedience, is endemic. It is fundamental to the human condition.

You can set up an operating procedure, and a certain fraction of the workforce is not going to follow it.

You can do abundant training (Driver's Education in the case of driving) but even at that, a certain fraction of the workforce is going to think that they are smarter than you. A certain fraction of the workforce will, unfortunately, be stupid. The combined number, based on a lot of different observations, is about 15%.

If this is part of the human condition, maybe you can keep out the riff raff. You, the hiring manager in some job that requires people to pay attention might be able to use this as a screening test. Maybe there is a correlation between irresponsible driving and irresponsible behavior of other types.

In most states driving records are considered in the public domain. In some other states, such as Georgia, you need the applicant's permission to access their driving records, so you can't check up on a job applicant.

Besides, this may be considered illegal in certain places because it is only considered "relevant" if your job involves a motor vehicle. Your 18-to 25-year-old male is going to complain since his female counterparts are less likely to be pulled over and ticketed for speeding.

Recurrent Patterns

As we go through a few of these ideas, we're going to see some recurrent patterns. The first one is, there are various reasons for people not doing their jobs properly.

Some of these are deeply rooted in human experience.

The second is that there are very often some underlying reasons why you can't screen these people out of the work force, a lot of them having to do with rules and laws of one kind or another.

There are detection and enforcement mechanisms which may or may not work. There are opportunities for automation which would reduce, but not completely eliminate the problem. There are ways to engineer lack of compliance out of the system. There are training methods.

But at the end of the day, some fraction of the workforce is not going to do their jobs. Your first lesson in Quality is to understand this, and deal with it constructively.

Or not. You could be like me and try to derive a revenue stream from it.

PS: Side point about the 1970's and early 1980's

At one point, during this era, due to a shortage of energy, the government imposed a 55-mph speed limit throughout the nation.

Did people obey that speed limit to any extent? This was so widely hated that despite the saving of many thousands of lives per year, and much energy, it was never again attempted.

This has been one of those issues that is a political thing now. One side has data that says it did nothing but slow people down and cost them money. Another said that it cost X number of lives per year in the decade after it was repealed, which was 1987.

https://youtu.be/moOv5adbm_I

Links and References

03 The Workforce is Impaired

A significant fraction of the workforce at a given moment is impaired in some way, and thus unable to do their jobs. We are going to review some statistics on this situation.

Historical References

Probably this has gone on since the invention of labor, or maybe the invention of impairment.

If you want to go back as far as Dickens, at the beginning of the industrial revolution, it looks like there was a sick, drunk population that was trying to survive in the world. There was no mass education, and life was fairly miserable for a lot of the population, if you believe Dickens.

If you want a further reference, you can go back to that scene in The Jungle, circa 1900 by Upton Sinclair. The meatpackers gave some of the child labor some of their lunch beer, with gruesome results.

Back in the Mad Men era, it was fairly common to have the "three martini lunch." Has this practice died out? No, I have to say it still exists in some places, and in some occupations. There are certain places, such as the dynamite factory, where this is a less good idea. I suppose if you are an office drone you don't think too much about it. If you're around heavy equipment it is not a good idea to be loaded.

I guess we could get into the fairness issue of why it is okay for some of the suits in the office to have a few beers over lunch, but not the fellow on the assembly line. But that's not what this is about.

This is about someone showing up wasted and not doing their job.

Personal Experience

There were a few instances through the years of me being in a dangerous place after chugging cold medicine, but I tried to keep out of the danger zone.

For a while, it was my job to take clients out to lunch and lubricate them a little. I am not going to pretend otherwise. Did this hurt anyone's productivity? I was a bit worried about a couple of them. Did it hurt my productivity? Well, if it was my job to do this, maybe not.

I made some videos a few years ago on this topic. Did the problem go away since then? No, I am ready to say that because of "long Covid" and a lot of other things that have happened since then, it may have gotten worse.

The reason this is important to you and I is that this is one of the many reasons that things aren't working right now. I have noticed this at all levels of the economy and across many different industries.

The Workforce Is Drunk or High

It is hard to put an exact number on this, because the publicly available statistics are not reliable. I've put a couple of recent references in the links and references. Somewhere between 5 and 15% of the employees in each work group drink, or get otherwise high, during the workday.

A significant fraction shows up at the start of the shift drunk or high.

The number seems to be highest in hospitality, namely bartenders or other alcohol-serving people. I'd drink too, if I were some of them.

Is this dangerous? I suppose, like we said above, that if the worker is some office drone that was a danger only to him or herself, it is harmless. But if the worker is some forklift operator moving drums of hydrochloric acid around the place, that is not a good thing.

Cultural Differences

I once had to go to a place not too far from Salzburg, which is in the lovely land of Austria. The factory was located in a beautiful mountain valley. It was December, a gentle, fluffy snow was coming down, and there were pretty little towns all around.

The factory itself was not especially beautiful but in this place, they were feeding the workforce comfort food. This consisted of lots of meat and potatoes for lunch. Along with that, the national drink, namely beer, was available free flowing. Was 15% of the workforce "loaded?" It was hard to say, but in that place maybe they're used to it.

We can go into the weird attitude toward drugs and alcohol in the US in some other book. For now, let's stick to the idea that it's probably not a good idea, in most companies in the US, to give free beer to the workers.

https://youtu.be/U21PAlUWUEo

The Workforce is Sleep Deprived

I don't believe the statistic in the references, which states that on a given day, 43% of the workforce is sleep deprived.

I think it's worse than that.

Any new parent is sleep deprived. 100% of the people on the night shift are sleep deprived. I was a night shift person for a while, and I can attest to it. In the places that work rotating shifts, 100% of the workforce is sleep deprived as well. No one can get on a fixed sleep schedule.

I am sleep deprived right now, as a matter of fact.

Sleep deprivation can cause all sorts of problems, including lack of concentration, loss of coordination, reduced reaction times, and mood disorders.

Over the long haul, it is a contributing factor to a lot of other metabolic diseases that can cause further workplace issues.

The Workforce is Impaired: They're Sick

According to the Bureau of Labor Statistics, at a given time, 1.5% of the workforce has called in sick. A similar enough percentage of the workforce is sick, but showed up anyway.

If the total of those things is 5%, that's one person out of a 20 person work group.

About 25% of the workforce in a given year had perfect attendance. I have a perfect attendance story for you. There was a hard headed production manager in the place where I worked right out of college, and he had "perfect attendance" for 45 years. Does that mean that he didn't get sick? No, of course not. It meant that he powered through it and contaminated everybody in the building.

Maybe we're a little wiser now.

They're Hurt

According to OSHA, the statistic was that 10.2 out of 100 workers got hurt back in 1972, and nowadays, this number has shrunk to about 2.7 workers out of 100.

This, we presume, would be the OSHA "Reportable" injury rate. That doesn't include the non-reportable injuries.

Keep in mind that in the USA, the percentage of the "non-farm" employment in manufacturing, which is known to be dangerous, has dropped by 50% in that time.

Depending on the job, it is likely that a fraction of the workforce at a given time is hurt and there are a lot of rules surrounding the Americans with Disabilities Act and "light duty" that suggests that a significant fraction is on the job at less than full strength.

I'm having trouble coming up with statistics for this, because the government data is outdated. Even AI does not have the exact answer.

According to the BLS, the "absenteeism rate" in the US in 2022 due to injury is 2.6%, and in addition the overall absenteeism rate is 3.8%, which in a work group is about one out of 30.

That doesn't include the people that are limping around the office in a walking boot because they twisted their ankle playing pickleball. I am going to walk around the issue of obesity for the moment. Obesity is so widespread right now that it might be a concurrent condition for most of these issues.

I am not ready to say that unless someone is a ballet dancer, obesity in and of itself is a reason for them not doing their job. However, I can be convinced otherwise. It is believed to be an element in being sick, having injuries, and having other medical conditions.

They're on Opiates
This was fairly shocking to me. 10% of the population, and I suppose the workforce, is walking around on painkillers. These are the legal painkillers, and don't include the illicit painkillers and other opiates that are prescribed at a rate of more than 100% of the population (that's right).

They're Stupid, have Psychological Issues and/or Personality Disorders
These things are enough of a concern that we're going to tackle them separately later on. Except according to

Bahnhover's Five Basic Laws of Human Stupidity, stupidity is independent of any other human condition.

It is likely that a certain fraction of the population is both stupid and has one of these other things going on.

Child or Elderly Care Issues

I am also going to briefly touch on the people not working because they have child care issues. A significant fraction of absenteeism is because their day care situation for that day fell through. This is a horrible problem, and probably the number is greater than the 104,000 people who lost work days per month that is cited in the references. That would be 0.6% give or take but among the group of workers I interact with, I believe it is higher than that.

Someone might be perfectly healthy but need to stay home for a sick dependent.

This is a significant stressor in various systems including the family system, and there is no good solution if we, as a society, want these people to work and do their jobs.

The Workplace is Using Social Media

At the time I did the accompanying video which was in the 2017–2018-time frame, it was estimated that 10% of the workforce was distracted by social media at any given time.

As of 2022, per the reference I have linked, it is estimated that up to 25% of drivers now are sending emails or texts while driving. I suppose it wouldn't be too much of a stretch to apply this to the workforce.

It is hard to get an actual number as to what fraction of these employees are distracted enough to cause peoples' jobs not to be done. If someone is streaming TikTok, they probably aren't doing their job.

The Workforce is Impaired

I suppose you can argue that none of these things is mutually exclusive. It's possible for one poor fellow to be drunk, sleep deprived, injured, strung out on opiates and streaming Netflix on the job.

But short of that, in a work group of 20, it is obvious. On a given walk through the production line or office or restaurant or another workplace, it's likely that half of them have something going on.

These are the people that are flipping your burgers, installing your toilets, or doing your demolition work. If not them, the people in the office, or bank or government. In a system where there is interdependence, like an assembly line, the whole thing shuts down at some point.

Why don't these people get fired?

Well, in some of the big industrial operations that I hang around in, they do.

But in a lot of little offices, or family businesses, or other smaller operations, they don't.

There is a list of reasons that people don't get fired, most of them associated with some relationship between the worker and the boss. I will add to these the ongoing labor force problems due to the pandemic and other issues that are going on in society.

I would refer you to my favorite talking head on the topic, Nicholas Eberstadt, who has written the book on this.

Men Without Work Book Link

https://www.amazon.com/Men-Without-Work-Post-Pandemic-Threats/dp/1599475979

My other favorite talking head on this topic is Mike Rowe, the Dirty Jobs guy.

Mike Rowe Video

https://www.youtube.com/watch?v=nfZGOMN8aF8

Because of current labor shortage issues, and because of the lack of people willing to get into some nasty field like toilet installation or manufacturing, people are more reluctant to fire someone even if they show up loaded.

I have a couple of references in the links and references about the whole issue of workplace drug screening, which was a big deal awhile back. It is less of a big deal because of the legalization of weed in certain areas of the US, raising the question that if someone shows up high on a legal drug, what can you or should you do about it?

Coping Strategies

There are a couple of coping strategies if you have the misfortune of being in charge of any of this.

The basic approach, if you are in a supervisory role, is to approach the employee carefully but directly, gather and present data, and set expectations. The HR department at your work, if there is one, may offer guidelines on this.

Keep in mind that use of some of these substances can be considered an indicator of a medical condition, which makes you, the manager, potentially exposing yourself and the company to liability issues. Someone in rehab has "protected status" and you may find yourself in a lawsuit if not careful.

As a co-worker, the main strategy seems to be to approach the fellow employee and ask if you can help. Keep in mind that the chances of you alienating the employee are greater than zero in a case like that. It is possible that if this is a workplace acquaintance, you can encourage them to seek professional guidance.

In either of these cases, excessive tolerance for employees showing up wasted might be considered a toxic workplace situation, and you may be better off hitting the road yourself. There is an apparent shortage of people who do their jobs.

The Workforce is Impaired

What I am saying is this:

In any given work group, there is an excellent chance that people are not doing their jobs because they are impaired.

In my opinion, backed up by statistics, this is on the order of 50/50.

We're living in a time where there is a strung out, sleep deprived, sick workforce. I believe this is a symptom of some underlying societal issues, but I also believe that there has been a certain amount of it since the dawn of time.

There are a lot of strategies to detect and deter this, but there may be limited success. In some cases, there are legal issues.

That doesn't necessarily help fix anything, but at least you are aware of the situation so that you can cope with it in whatever way you can.

Links and References

04 How to Develop a Terrible Workforce

In the spirit of Deming, we're going to take on the project of workforce development, namely how to develop a terrible workforce. Deming says that a system is perfectly engineered to produce what it does. So, if the system has already produced a workforce that doesn't show up for work, is illiterate and untrainable, can't do creative problem solving and when they do show up, they're drunk or high, it should be easy to figure out how we, as a society, managed to do this, and start doing the opposite, if we want a workforce that is high functioning.

Importance of Workforce Development

An essential element in people not doing their jobs is a workforce, at all levels, that is capable of work. We're not really asking for rocket science, unless, of course, we need to make rockets.

Basic Assumptions

We probably should have covered this in the introduction.

Our focus assumes that we're working on managing some kind of economic entity. The extreme example is a giant manufacturing plant, with 5000 or more employees, and the other extreme example is the ice cream place down at the strip mall, with a handful of employees.

We, as a species, started to need this kind of organization a long time ago. I will leave it to you to come up with the date of the first workforce and figure out how long ago the first workplace screw-up was. Archaeologists of today are questioning everything we've "learned" about civilization.

What we are primarily interested in is the kind of workforce that we've needed since the dawn of the Industrial Revolution. We're skipping over the apprentice system, and the system of specialized workers, that apparently started, ironically, at about the same time beer was invented.

We can study those societies later.

The Age of Enlightenment and Horace Mann
The Age of Enlightenment happened over a period of a couple of centuries and started mainly in Europe.

It was a set of attitudes centered on human happiness, decision making based on reason, separation of Church and State, and other aspects of civilization that helped things to function.

The people we call the "founding fathers" of the USA were all disciples of this, and the basic concepts have spread widely, but not everywhere. Some people would prefer not to be "enlightened." The Founding Fathers valued education, but not enough to make it a human right.

As it applied to the Industrial Revolution, it became pretty obvious that we, as a society, could make our industry more efficient if we had a way to do "workforce development." The leading proponent of this in the USA was Horace Mann, who felt like it was the government's job to finance this system.

The intent of this system was to have a standardized way of screening to keep out the riff raff. He arranged the classrooms in a way that resembled a sweatshop, inflicted punishment, and otherwise got people ready for factory life. At the time, that was considered a good thing, and the first "students" were the little mill girls who were indoctrinated into the system.

In the rural areas, which most of the country was at that point, the curriculum was adjusted to meet the needs of that community.

https://youtu.be/zcLuVLQq1YM

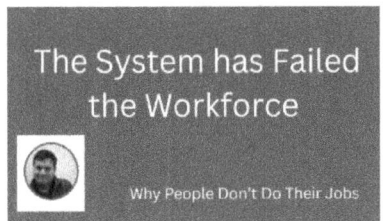

The System has Failed the Workforce

Why People Don't Do Their Jobs

Problems with This Plan

There were several underlying problems with this plan. It was, in its way, brutal, it did not adapt to individual learning styles, and most of all, we couldn't, and still can't, come to agreement on what it means to be "educated."

This was a special hot potato in the areas of the country that still had slavery. In those areas, there was an underlying hostility toward people paying taxes so that other peoples' kids could get an education. This also trickles down to today.

The System in 1960

I am using this as a proposed year for the ultimate expression of this system. This was the era of the nice schoolhouse, full of baby boomers. They sat in the corner or did detention if they acted up. There was a flag in the front, and a stern Principal, and a board of education, which inflicted corporal punishment. You got a report card, which you were expected to show your parents, and for the most part, they expected competence.

They knew at the time that the model was not equally good for everybody so there was shop class and auto mechanics. When you got a diploma, it meant that you tolerated 12 years of the system. The kids that were going to college were picked out, and everybody knew their place in the social dominance hierarchy.

The parents tended to support the system, even though it had its nuances. If you were sure your little boy or girl was college material, there were alternate paths through the system. Was there bullying, discrimination, people acting badly? Yes, there was. The system was far from perfect.

Across the southeast schools were gradually being desegregated. Segregation was made illegal in 1955 but it took 20 years for some of these places to get the message. We found out the other day that in Louisville, which is pretty far north, it only happened in 1975. That is a can of worms. We will never know what human potential was lost because of this. Some of these places are just as badly segregated now as they were at the time.

Did any of this Help?

The product of this whole process, the labor force circa 1960, was perfectly capable of stepping into a work situation. They were also perfectly capable of packing an M-16 into a rice paddy, because these "skills" which included following orders and not making waves are also beneficial for the military.

The Horace Mann system was also invented based on the Prussian system, which was all about providing cannon fodder for that lovely country's many ongoing wars.

1974 was the maximum year of everything in the US. Since that time, the inflation-adjusted per capita income in the country has gone down for the bottom ⅔ of the population. There were some signs of instability in the few years before or after that. There is a statistical link below, the peak was "percentage of the population completing high school", although we will not be able to agree whether these kids learned anything special. The peak of that was 1974.

How to Develop a Terrible Workforce: Early Childhood Development

If we are to begin a project to create the least effective workforce possible, we have to start early. We have to deprive infants and babies of nutrition, motherly care, and a safe environment.

There is a statistical correlation between breastfeeding and IQ, so I suppose we would do away with that. However, part of breastfeeding is to have a present mother, rather than one who dumps the infant off in day care to do her low wage job, so there is not necessarily causation.

The difference between causation and correlation, by the way, is an important idea that we should avoid teaching at all, if we are going to develop a workforce without critical thinking skills.

We should expose infants to heavy metals. According to some research, these intellect-killing substances are in the water and land, in some places. We should also feed them a steady diet of as much sugar as possible.

We should deprive them of two-parent families. According to the statistics in the links and references, 23% of kids are brought up in single parent families. Only about 63% of kids are brought up in homes with both of their biological parents.

Of the kids who spend time with dad, 75% eventually go on to have stable employment, so we'd have to get dad out of the picture. Kids who had fatherhood time are more emotionally stable, and have higher levels of sociability and self-control, according to research. I am not saying alternate methods of raising kids is bad, but these are people who hear the word "no" occasionally.

If we want to try to cripple the workforce, there should be a lot of anti-dad policies enacted.

School Days
We have to start with the teachers.

I spent some time exploring the myth that most teachers in this era come from the bottom third of their college class. There is no real data to back that up. However, there is some IQ data which I have referenced that says that the typical teacher IQ is 85-115, which means that teachers are no smarter than the so-called "average" employee.

Jordan Peterson has the idea that the US Military will reject people that have IQ under 83, because they are considered untrainable.

Jordan Peterson ref; IQ

https://www.youtube.com/watch?v=5-Ur7iZnNVk&t=66s/

There are other references that suggest that the military doesn't measure IQ but does reject the bottom ⅓ of applicants based on some other standardized testing. That being the case, there is a fraction of the population who will be rejected by the US military for being unintelligent but hired as a schoolteacher.

If we were to engineer a system to fail, that would be a good start. Maximize those people. A system of preferentially hiring the unintelligent to be schoolteachers would be perfect.

Teacher Pay

According to the references, the typical starting pay for a parking lot attendant in Atlanta is $13.60 per hour. The minimum starting pay for an elementary school teacher in Atlanta is $12.50 per hour, but you don't have to have a college education or a teaching certificate to sit around and attend to peoples' cars.

So, it looks like this system is well on its way to discouraging new teachers and ensuring that our cars are safe. Barely.

I think the average salary for a baggage handler at the Atlanta Airport is around $15 an hour, but those people have worse hours and must lift baggage.

To be perfectly fair, the average annual teacher pay in Atlanta is closer to $60K, but the average engineer pay is $95K. So, if you're bright enough to be an engineer, there is plenty of incentive for you to ditch the idea of being a teacher. Can you predict that your teacher is less smart than an engineer? Maybe not. Some people are dedicated to shaping young minds.

Should it matter that 80% of the elementary school teachers are female? If we want to maximize the culture shock of having to deal with a male authority figure when the kids start their jobs, we should get it all the way up to 100%.

55% of the teaching force at the moment is ready to quit. 40% of the "regular workforce" at the moment is ready to quit as well, so the incidence is a little higher for teachers.

Role of the School

At some point, the role of the school has evolved. At first, it started to be a place where kids could go to learn content. Now, it has evolved into a multi-level care system. The kids can eat breakfast and lunch there, and a significant portion of kids now rely on this as a source of nutrition.

This expanded greatly in 1966, and if you're below the poverty line the school system will now pay to feed you.

In a lot of areas, there is a school-based mental health system which diagnoses and tries to treat mental health issues. That also used to be the job of the parents.

There are 2500 school medical clinics throughout the country to detect and diagnose illnesses of one kind or another. That also mainly used to be the job of the parents.

Does anybody think that since these programs were put into place the workforce has gotten better? It is hard to come up with hard data, but it looks like it has mainly kept it from being worse. We still have to tackle the problem of measurements and accountability.

Measurements and Accountability

Deming would say, you can't improve what you don't measure. We as a society still are not completely together on what it means to be educated.

The ideal situation would be one of standardized testing, which had in it a certain amount of content that was deemed central to a productive workforce. Ideally this should be designed by business owners, and include some technical content, communication, basic problem solving, including math, and a student could and should be ranked on the basis of it.

This was invented by Horace Mann but reached its apex in the early 2000's when "no child left behind" was enacted.

For those wanting to destroy the system, just do away with all of that. Whine because it is biased against certain people. Eliminate test results as a requirement to move on to college. Encourage school systems to cheat, like they did in Atlanta a few years ago.

Then, dumb down the curriculum, and do away with truth telling as it applies to kids. Be sure not to hurt anyone's feelings. Give everybody a trophy. Teach content so that it is as inoffensive as possible, and have the teachers be a delivery device for the information. Expect them to think as little as possible. Have educational content decided by whichever special interest group is the most vocal at the moment, even if they are a minority in the community.

Don't have minimal nationwide standards. After all, if a community chooses to raise generation after generation of idiots, it should be allowed to, right?

School Choice

If you have a select group of "elite" students, provided you want the system to fail, make sure to get them out of the system. Send them to "magnet schools" or out of public education altogether. Allow the rest of the kids whose parents can't afford to truck their kids across town to sink or swim on their own.

Students learning from each other is a trend under the supposition that in some statistically predictable percentage of the time, the kids are smarter than the teachers. We can't have them near the dunderheads who we want to keep helpless.

If you still want to spend tax money on a vast, undereducated population, you can do so. If you're going to maximize the number of kids that are warehoused in underachieving schools, then remove the smart kids. Make it a culture of mediocrity.

Home schooling? I guess that's where you opt out of the system entirely and have your mom (usually it's your mom) "educate" you. How is that working out? Well since we have no way to measure, there's no way to tell as it applies to its effects on the workforce. There is a reference that talks all about correlation and causation, which is something a homeschooler might know if their mom knew statistics.

One more thing: If you want to produce a failing workforce, whatever you do, don't put them on a farm. Farm kids are used to solving problems, working their asses off and integrating into the workforce. If you want to produce a culture of failure, this is the opposite of what you want.

College

We're not even going to try to figure this out at the moment. The US system of higher education is, in the words of the article that I have linked, reviled at home but the envy of the world. But it's a system where kids are going into massive debt to get credentials in fields of study where they can't get jobs.

In our project to develop the worst workforce possible, we'll leave them alone for the moment.

What if some of these kids show up at the factory door looking for work? Your guess is as good as mine. It depends on the kid, I suppose.

How to Change Any of This?

Well, we're in a bit of a pickle when it comes to changing any sort of system right now.

We're all trauma survivors when it comes to the medical and pharmaceutical system, aren't we? Complex systems in this period can't be changed without a lot of argument, and there is an army of lobbyists and special interests with handfuls of "campaign contributions" to keep it from being changed.

The same things can be said about the air travel, railroad, corporate governance and food production and delivery systems. They're practically impossible to change at a high level. Every "tax reform" results in the tax code being even fatter, and the benefits not widely spread out.

So, it is with the childhood development and education system. There are constituencies to deal with, including publishers, teachers' unions, local government officials, and others who like the system the way it is.

That is one of the definitions of "entrenched mediocrity" that we're going to explore at some point. There is a system with known deficiencies that can't be changed, even though we think we can do better.

To change the educational system, as we keep finding out, you have to change the thousands of little local communities who have their own biases and special interests. Any proposed change is likely to be watered down by the political process and eventually neutered.

So even if we tried to make it worse, on its own, we'd be hard pressed to find a way to do it. No one is in charge. There's no button to push.

The Result

With a lot of work, by tinkering with the system like we suggested above, you could end up with a vast, undereducated workforce. They won't listen to instruction, they'll communicate improperly, they won't show up to work, and blow up and quit over minor issues. You won't be able to correct them via feedback. They'll show up to meetings late, have no initiative, always be on the phone and require constant supervision.

They won't do their jobs.

Can you completely attribute any of this to the educational system? Not without attributing it to society in general. I guess that's the point. The system, whether societal or educational, has failed the workforce.

Like we said, a system is perfectly set up to produce what it does.

The best we can do now is try to derive a revenue stream from it.

Links and References

Why People Don't Do Their Jobs

05 The Workplace is Toxic

We're going to talk about a situation now where the workplace is toxic. Now, we don't mean that people are exposed to toxic chemicals, or other hazardous conditions. We're talking about a situation where you're working with a lot of backstabbers and liars that make employees not want to do their jobs.

We can probably talk about the toxic chemicals later. That still exists in some places but is not as bad as it was 50 years ago when I entered the workforce.

What we're talking about now is a work environment where it is socially annoying to show up to the office. The bigger the company, the more likely this is to happen, but it is not unheard of in startups or other organizations.

Disclaimer

I am going to use a farmyard term in the discussion below. Being from Iowa, like I am, I am not embarrassed by this. I would not normally do so, as those who I have worked with know, but in this case, it is a useful word because people can read into it what they want. It can describe something harmless but annoying, and it can describe something toxic and intolerable. It is contextual.

That's why it is such an interesting word, and the non-English speakers that hear it will have to look for a similar word in their own language. I am using it very deliberately for exactly this reason.

Anyway, if you are offended by that word, you should go on to the next chapter. In fact, that is partly the point of this.

Different people have different levels of tolerance for being offended.

Definition of a Toxic Workplace

The Wikipedia definition of a Toxic Workplace is one which has significant personal conflicts between the people that work there. Quite often, this happens in an office environment.

Co-workers are distracted by gossip, workplace violence, emotional abuse and other antisocial behavior. There is a certain amount of this anytime there are people working with people. We're talking about a situation where it is serious enough that people aren't doing their jobs.

One of the problems with this is that it is in the eye of the beholder, and the definition of this is shifting over time. There is a fine line between some workplace banter and teasing and harassment. We're going to have to find some examples.

Signs of a Toxic Workplace

It's easier to make a list of features of a toxic workplace than it is to define it concisely. There are a couple of references that have given us some examples of workplace toxicity.

Here are some examples.

Condition	Effect on People Doing Their Jobs
Overwork and Work Life Balance	"Work Quality" to the extent it can be defined is poor.
High Turnover	New people are always being trained, there are ongoing performance issues
People Don't Trust Each Other (including the Boss)	Work is wasted, meaningless work is done, and work is not rewarded properly, thus ticking people off.
Lack of Communication	There is wasted effort, since it is not clear what peoples' jobs are.
There is no room for mistakes	Mistakes are not taken as training opportunities so there is covering up, and no improvement.
People hate each other	Work is destroyed or degraded; work is allowed

	to pile up. There may be sabotage.
No employee support	Employees are impaired, injured and otherwise can't function productively
Role Confusion	Employees worry about expectations, there may be lack of agreement on performance measurements, Conflict can arise between workers (Loafers are tolerated.)
Physical symptoms of work stress	Employees do not show up, get sick, are ticked off and don't do their jobs.
Excessive Office Gossip	Employees lose teamwork and productivity suffers.

None of this is easy to define quantitatively. Let's take the last one for example. There is an informal communication network in every workplace of more than two people. This may be communication about someone's physical condition, something going on in someone's outside life, and other information that might be helpful from the standpoint of mutual support.

Informal communication is a fact of life in any place where there are humans.

But when it gets to the point at which it becomes harmful, and hurts productivity, then people are gossiping instead of doing their jobs. The same goes for many of these other issues. There is no clear line as to what "too much" is.

Banana Time

The best article I ever saw on this was linked in the links and references; it's called "Banana Time" by Donald F. Roy. It was originally published in 1959, in the Journal of Applied Anthropology. I guess that is what we're talking about. Human culture as it is applied in the workplace.

It talked about a work group in a very monotonous activity that developed an informal workplace culture, which included teasing, gossip, and other workplace banter. The writer, who was a college student at the time, observed that this informal office culture was a way to improve job satisfaction. It was a "good thing" and there were self-imposed limits.

Emotional Resilience

Jordan Peterson, current talking head, has an excellent example of informal workplace culture:

Lunch Bucket

https://www.youtube.com/watch?v=FzM7pa1HuCY/

Resilience Testing

https://youtu.be/d2NEnEPgMIM?si=BaW9lUBcwVA95bAg

It describes workplace banter which was done within a work group on a railroad crew. I can relate to this strongly because I was on exactly such a type of railroad crew, approximately 600 miles south of there.

Peterson looks at this as serving several social functions. It is a way for the work group to test an individual, to see what their tolerance for discomfort is. It is a way to initiate play and determine whether the "target" is properly socialized. If the work group found out that the person was untrustworthy or had other issues, it is an informal way of sorting all of that out.

This further clip from the Jocko Willink podcast further illustrates this:

More Resilience Tests

https://youtu.be/futHL4W4E4s?si=76cvYsnmfM6ah9wP

Workplace Banter

"Workplace banter" goes on all the time. At what point does it become a "toxic work environment?"

Whether a workplace is toxic or not depends on two things: The tolerance of a given employee to toxicity, and existing toxicity in the workplace, as defined somehow.

For the moment, let's equate "toxicity" and something we in the USA call "bullshit."

The Bullshit Tolerance Bell Curve

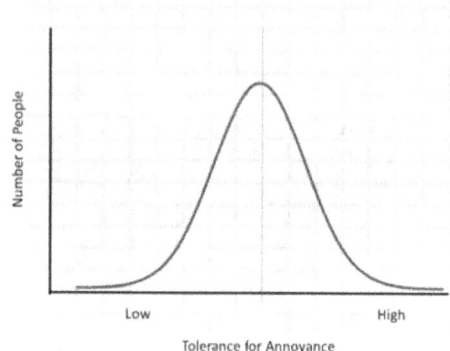

Tolerance for Annoyance

You will recognize this as a normal distribution curve. On the vertical axis is the number of people, and along the horizontal axis is the tolerance for bullshit. This could be for an individual, a work group, or society in general.

Bullshit is a term that deserves a book of its own. Bullshit comes in four main varieties: Physical bullshit, emotional bullshit, technological bullshit, and bureaucratic bullshit. There are more types, of course, but these are the main ones.

So, let's say that a given workforce, or a given individual, is willing to put up with a certain amount of bullshit.

Here is an annotated version of this graph:

69

Normal (Whatever that is)

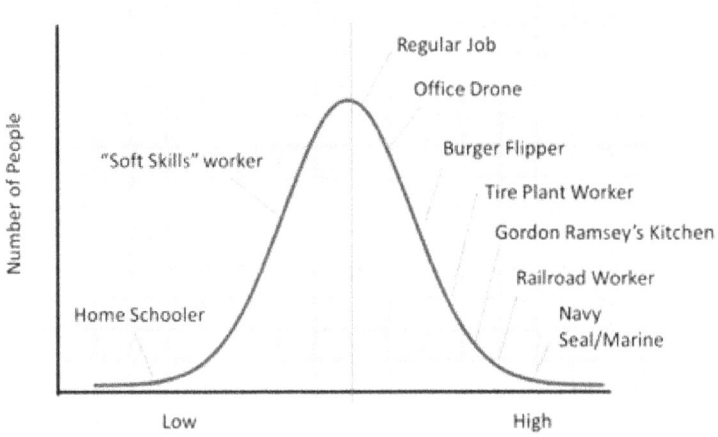

They will say "This is bullshit," and stomp off. There may be an adverse event, or maybe they'll just leave for lunch and not come back.

Across the horizontal axis, there may be different levels of tolerance for different types of bullshit. For example, your railroad worker may find it easy to cope with physical bullshit, but not be able to fill out his timecard. That is fine, you may draw a separate curve for each type of bullshit if you want.

However, this graph explains why there aren't very many Navy Seals. They are highly trained to have a high tolerance for bullshit (physical, emotional and danger). The same can be said for Jordan Peterson's railroad worker, or someone who tries to work in Gordon Ramsey's kitchen.

In fact, the reason Gordon Ramsey treats his workers like he does is to test their resilience. Most people have been through tests of resilience of one type or another. The

70

"average office drone" or "normal worker" is somewhere in the middle, so there are a lot more of them. There is a certain percentage of the workforce that is intolerant of bullshit. These are the highly sensitive people, who burst into tears when someone looks at them funny in the workplace.

All workplaces have a certain amount of bullshit. A good manager will look for ways to reduce the amount of bullshit his or her employees must put up with. A terrible manager will add to the bullshit. If the bullshit level gets too high, there will be workforce dysfunction. The "average person" won't put up with it.

If you want to substitute the phrase "workplace toxicity" for "bullshit" you may do so.

Bullshit Variance Over Time
Here are a couple more graphs:

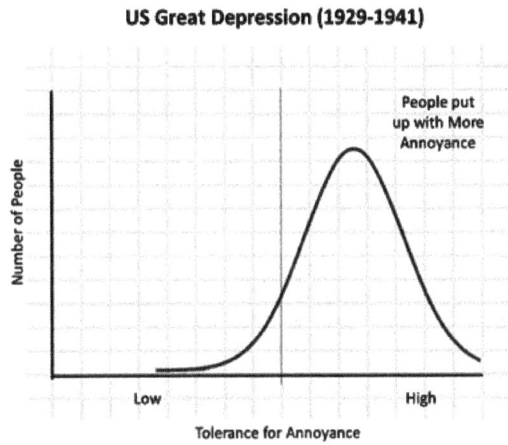

In the US Great Depression, and in other periods of economic dislocation, there is a shift of this bullshit tolerance to the right. If people are having trouble finding jobs, they will be much more tolerant of bullshit than they otherwise would. You'll find a lot more people willing to work as a tire plant worker, or office drone. A lot of super-sensitive people will end up unemployed because they can't tolerate bullshit.

It works the same way in the Great Resignation, which is probably still going on. Because of PTSD, Covid, and other factors, people are much less tolerant of bullshit than they used to be, which is why there are shortages of employees in industries such as tire plant workers and burger flippers. The Amazon fulfillment people are in that same range.

Everyone wants to stay home rather than put up with bullshit.

The Great Resignation (2020-2022)

Tolerance for Annoyance

It also explains why there are so many super-sensitive people right now.

This Explains Several Things

As it applies to the toxic workplace: There is a reason that your grandparents have no idea what a Toxic Workplace was. All workplaces were toxic, and during the Depression Era, people put up with what they had to.

It also shows that as people get closer to retirement, they are less and less willing to put up with bullshit.

It also explains why some workplaces start out as reasonable, and over time become toxic. Your old crusty manager will say "people don't want to work anymore" but can't recognize that the tolerance of people for bullshit is a lot less than it was when they started the business.

And, if your boss was from a generation where a good butt chewing once or twice a week was appropriate behavior, you can imagine their confusion in this era, where the workforce will no longer tolerate it.

https://youtu.be/14wLgtIJauk

Culture Fit

It also explains why "culture fit" is critically important. Are you going to take a squishy soft skills worker, and drop them into the middle of Gordon Ramsey's kitchen? No, you aren't. In fact, the producers of the show make it interesting because they do just that. They deliberately put these people into that environment hoping that they'll get upset, burst into tears, and stomp off.

74

Are you going to take a railroad worker and stick them into a work group of soft skills people? Physical differences aside, it is likely that due to the temperament of the typical railroad worker, they'll wander off out of boredom, or be a "contributor" of bullshit to the poor employees in the "soft skills" department. That might be the more interesting reality show.

Bullshit and Reward

There is a certain type of employee that will put up with an immense amount of bullshit if they are well rewarded. I worked in an organization at one point with a boss who was a source of bullshit, rather than a recipient. His way of dealing with workplace toxicity was to pile on more of it, and reward people for putting up with it.

This fellow was the President of the Company, who had four Vice Presidents. All the Vice Presidents had heart attacks or strokes at some point. That, readers, is the very definition of a toxic workplace. Why did they put up with it? Well for them, the pay and status were worth it.

Would this boss have been more effective by making these fellows' jobs easier? Quite possibly, if the employees were talented enough. But in one of these organizations maybe the main talent was their ability to put up with the boss. We will never know. All of them are long gone now.

College and Other Rites of Passage

Do you get that this is why college has some merit? You can get exactly the same content as college, probably even better, by reading blog posts or books like this one.

In fact, I'm ready to say that this is better than a lot of the college lectures I sat through, if I do say so. But what you don't get is experience in dealing with bullshit. There are prerequisites, and requirements, and double secret probation, and advisor meetings, and a lot of other overhead activities that the college deems necessary and add nothing to the content of your college education. However, they do teach you how to deal with bullshit.

If you don't want to take out student loans for the purpose of your diploma you may decline to do so. But when you apply for a job in a complex organization, you would have some proof that you can put up with a ration of bullshit. That's what your diploma really is, you know.

The same can be said for the Social Security system, US Military, Legal system and a lot of other systems we are aware of.

Putting Yourself through Adversity

This is another thing that is happening. People realize that society overall has gotten progressively softer. This is because people are no longer involved in farming or manufacturing that would have presented them with mental or physical adversity.

These are the people that are marathon runners, cross country bikers, naked mountain climbers and the like. The main idea is that by doing these things, in absence of other rites of passage, they are increasing their tolerance for bullshit, which is a useful thing to do.

These people can navigate the workplace, put up with a little discomfort, and do other activities that we used to call "character building." The same might be said for Navy Seals, provided they tolerate the paperwork.

Toxic Individuals

There are such people as toxic individuals. These are people that, because of their personal characteristics, cause the people around them to flip out and not do their jobs. Are toxic individuals made, or born? I have seen a few examples of both.

It's best not to have these people in the workforce. Either figure out a way to screen them out or fire them. Keep in mind that if you can't tell who the most toxic person in the workplace is, it's probably you. If you are the manager, so much the worse.

The Workplace is Toxic

"Toxic Workplace" is a product of the conditions, and the people in it.

When the tolerance of the workforce or individual is exceeded, job dysfunction occurs. No one wants that. People don't do their jobs.

The good managers are aware of this and are on the lookout for ways to reduce the amount of "toxicity" that is "bullshit" that the labor force must deal with. The bad managers add to it.

If you have the misfortune of being in a toxic workplace yourself, you may realize that you are not properly fitted into your job. Your two choices, take it or leave it, are dependent on your personal condition, tolerance for bullshit, and the reward system that got you into that situation and is keeping you there.

Links and Reference

06 People Are Ticked Off

We're now going to tackle the topic of people being Ticked Off. Employee anger, as well as other personality and mental disorders, are a major reason why people don't do their jobs.

Ticked off, as the Urban Dictionary hilariously tells us, is an intermediate stage of anger midway between "miffed" and "pissed off."

The effects of people being ticked off, or having other personality disorders, vary a lot depending on where in the organization they are, and whether their performance is helped or hurt by being angry.

How Widespread is this Problem?

According to "Mind your anger dot com," from the British Association of Anger Management, ⅓ of the people polled have a friend or family member that has a problem controlling anger. 12% of the population at a given time admit to having an anger problem themselves, and they strongly recommend taking an "anger retreat" to some lovely, sunny spot like Malaga.

According to Forbes, which quotes the Gallup organization, 81% of the workforce is "burned out" and 44% of global employees experienced anger or anxiety "a lot" the previous day.

The problem is severe enough that Starbucks is citing this as a reason for closing stores, in that both employees and customers are experiencing "incidents." Caffeine may be a gateway drug.

The original report from the Gallup organization, who has put out their annual "State of the Global Workplace" is linked in the links and references. That thing says that at the present time, the "daily anger" rate in North America is 18%. Which means that of the five people you see sitting around a table in the cafeteria, one of them is "angry." Whether or not that rises to the point of being "ticked off" is an open question, but it is not an especially good sign.

https://youtu.be/2ziqunQh9SA

They're Ticked Off

Why People Don't Do Their Jobs

Negative Effects of Anger

Most sources cite effects such as anxiety, decreased productivity, and potentially sabotage. An article from the Wharton School suggests that being angry clouds your judgment, which makes for potential bad decision making.

Going Postal

According to the NIMH, 10% of the "angry population" also has firearms in their homes, and 1.6% of the anger trait people carry firearms outside the home. All I can say to that is, that I hope it's that low.

Statista provides a list of 53 "incidents" that are workplace-related over the last few years. The phrase "going postal" has entered the language to describe workplace firearm incidents, especially in a repetitive job. Enterprise Apps states that there were 400,000 aggravated assaults in the workplace. 68% of employees do not feel safe in their workplace.

Dealing with an Angry Boss

This is a particularly sticky issue and there is a lot in the literature about it. As an employee, you'd love to be treated with respect, consideration, support, and a positive work environment.

But 52% of workers are currently ready to change jobs because of the boss. I have linked to a forum that describes some of these experiences.

Particularly annoying is the type of boss who kisses up to the higher levels of the organization but treats his or her employees like garbage.

For one thing, keep in mind that a boss is a person too, and is equally likely, and in fact maybe more likely, to have anger issues or other personal issues that he or she takes out on the employees.

This, unfortunately, is not going away.

There is an article linked from Business Insider which describes 26 characteristics of a "bad boss." These include lying, cheating, withholding information and a lot of other activities which destroy employee morale, and other behavior which contribute to a screwed-up work environment, and also threaten your home environment.

Here's a book reference. I can't be more authoritative on how to deal with this topic than this.

Bad Bosses, Crazy Co Workers and Other Office Idiots

https://www.amazon.com/gp/product/1402212534

How does this affect People Doing Their Jobs?

It would be another good topic for a PhD dissertation if someone would tackle the project of putting a dollar amount on this. For one thing, it's a workplace distraction, and we all know distractions are bad. We know it's widespread enough to cause laws to be passed, and we, as a society, are limited as to how to deal with it.

Yet another PhD dissertation would be to come up with a dollar amount of improved quality and improved productivity because of a happy workforce. There is for sure some numbers around to capture the cost of re-hiring a worker that was ticked off and quit, and it can be up to

33% of a worker's salary. We'll have a little more to say about this later.

Turnover and unmotivated employees are expensive.

My favorite "Angry Boss" story.

I worked in a place in Texas, with a fellow who was "Texas Angry."

Texas, probably like New Jersey, is a place where a lot of people walk around and as part of their persona, act angry. It's sort of aggressive, in a Texas sort of way. You have to have been there to experience it.

The "Rich Texan" character in The Simpsons is sort of like that. This is angry in the same way a football coach, or a drill sergeant would be "angry" at you. They behave that way for effect.

This fellow was a production supervisor and would blow up several times a day just to communicate to the people around him, who were 90% immigrants that didn't understand English.

This fellow was so angry one time that he threw his hat in the middle of the floor, and for three days, the employees drove the sweeper around that hat because everyone was afraid to touch it.

We never knew whether he was pretending to be angry or he was angry. After working there for a few years, he gradually started to reveal that he had a personality. He was almost friendly, and eventually he was declared "disabled" because of chronic dust overexposure, which we all had. He had also been in Korea in 1951. Maybe he was "giving up."

Did that guy get people to do their jobs? Well, maybe for that place and time and culture, he did, but paid the price, as did the people around him. It's hard to live like that.

Other Personality Disorders

According to the NIMH Personality disorders represent "an enduring pattern of inner experience and behavior that deviates markedly from the expectations of the individual's culture." And the prevalence of this in the workplace is around 10%.

If you suspect that your workforce has a lot of crazy people in it, you're right. If you add this to the half of the workforce from the previous chapter who are impaired, it's no wonder things don't get done.

According to Champion Health, the prevalence of mood disorders, including depression, anxiety and stress is as high as 60%, and 15% of the workforce rises to the level of needing treatment. They suggest that it's a good idea to try to spot some of these people, and deal with them constructively.

Symptoms of Psychological Disorders

These symptoms are not always obvious, but there are common signs to look out for. Here are 10 things to look out for when it comes to spotting mental health issues at work:

Uncharacteristic behavior

Low levels of engagement

Decreases in productivity

Changes in sleeping or eating behaviors

Disinterest in work or day-to-day activities

Increased absence

Changes in working patterns

Withdrawal from social situations

Irrational fears, paranoia or anxiety

Substance use/misuse

The "uncharacteristic behavior" is an interesting phrase. What is "uncharacteristic" exactly? Some people are characteristically a little weird.

I also want to know whose job it is to approach someone sitting alone in the corner of the cafeteria, gritting his or her teeth every day at lunchtime, wearing an NRA hat. Are you doing that? Not me.

Mental Health Story

I worked in a place on the evening shift. There was a fellow that worked in the inspection department as a supervisor. I will tell you later what he was inspecting. His name was Jim.

I guess you would have to say that he was chronically angry, but in a comical way, like Granny in the Beverly Hillbillies. We had an evening quality meeting and the Technical Service guy, and I would go down to the meeting room a little early every night to see if we could get him wound up. He was a small guy, maybe 5' 5" and weighing about 120 pounds.

As I think I said before, most of the "old guys" I used to work for are younger than I am right now. Jim was in that category. He might have been in his late 50's.

86

He loved to complain about his sons-in-law, who were apparently giants, and could eat an entire refrigerator full of food in one sitting. He'd hilariously tell the stories and get "agitated." I think he liked the attention.

He also had chronic issues with sore feet. His job was to walk around on concrete all the time. We guessed that he had been in the plant for 20 years, and that was also bothering him. He walked around like someone with sore feet. He also complained about his tyrant boss giving him a hard time. In those days, bosses had to be tyrants.

We also, over a period, found out that he had spent several months on Guadalcanal. If you aren't aware of the seriousness of this, I have provided a link in the links and references. But to make a long story short, it is very likely he also had the condition that we now call PTSD. He also looked out the corner of his eye and gritted his teeth at the Japanese employee at the next station.

So, from his point of view, chronic physical pain, domestic issues, PTSD, and no one around him giving him any sort of sympathy, life was unbearable. That being the case, he ended it. They had the service at 10 AM so that the second shift employees that worked for him could attend.

In his case, what, if anything, could have or should have been done? Was he functioning properly in his job, as it was? I suppose you would have to say he was, but there was no one in the system that would or could have done something, including me and the tech service guy.

Why aren't these people fired?
One of the lessons is, a person can go for a long time with one or more of these issues, and still do their jobs. In fact, in the case of OCD it might help you in some positions.

But mostly, firing someone with a mental condition is illegal.

The US Department of Labor states that mental health issues are considered a "disability" and an employer in the US is required to provide "reasonable accommodation" and other rules regarding this as a physical and mental condition.

On the US department of labor website, there's a video about mental health in the Federal workplace:

Federal Government Mental Health

https://youtu.be/OuJBkgfD9vQ?si=nR19zvg_YI7XBzRX

In fact, these conditions are also covered under the HIPAA rules, which state that you can't disclose "publicly" the fact that a person has these conditions. So even if you, the HR person or manager, know that someone is a bit off, you're subject to up to a $100,000 fine and a year in the joint if you don't protect this information.

Workplace Anger

As part of the human condition, some people are chronically angry. They may have other chronic mental health and emotional issues that keep them from doing their job. The incidence of this is widespread. About 15 to 20% of the population, if the statistics are to be believed.

These people are a drain on productivity, make bad decisions, and often screw up the professional and personal lives of the people around them. Not always though, sometimes you can't even tell. These are the "silent angry."

Can you, as a participant in the workplace, learn anything from this? I'd say sure. Be careful. You never know who is packing heat.

<u>Links and References</u>

07 Employees are Disengaged

We're now talking about the ongoing "crisis" of employees being disengaged. Employee engagement is where an employee is enthusiastically dedicated to their job and their co-workers. Employee disengagement is the opposite of that. The employee is indifferent or hostile to their job and co-workers.

The leading current authority on this topic is the Gallup Organization, who has taken a priceless survey on the topic of the workplace for several years now. I have linked it again for your reference.

https://youtu.be/oBqoU_IvcGk

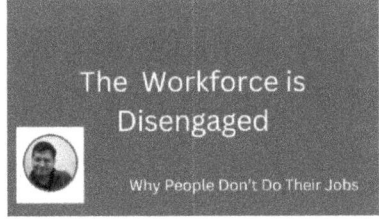

Disengagement Statistics

The Gallup Organization conducts an annual survey about the state of the workplace in the US and a variety of other industrialized nations.

According to the survey, in North America only 31% of the workforce as of late last year is "engaged" in their jobs, and 17% of the workforce is considered "actively disengaged" which is to say, walking around the office trying to spread the misery.

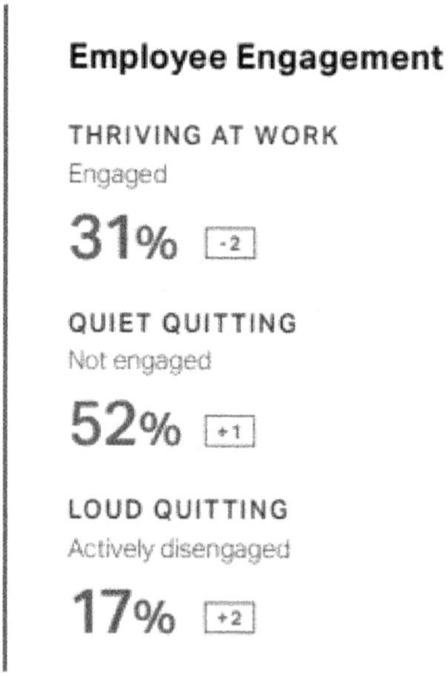

Employee Engagement

THRIVING AT WORK
Engaged

31% `-2`

QUIET QUITTING
Not engaged

52% `+1`

LOUD QUITTING
Actively disengaged

17% `+2`

The survey equates "disengagement" which is otherwise defined as doing the bare minimum at work with the phenomenon of "quiet quitting."

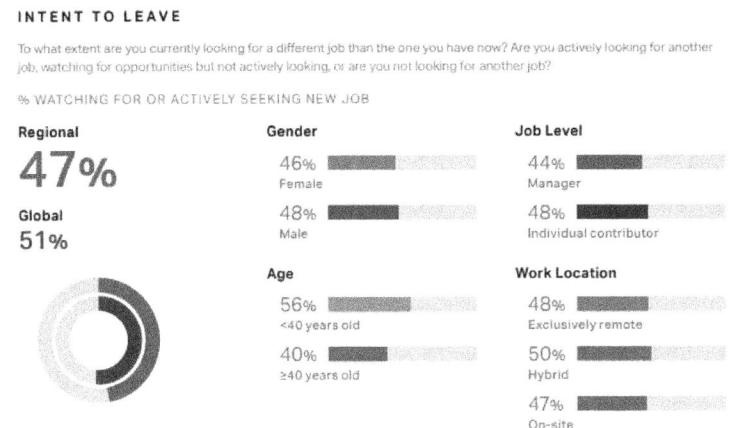

INTENT TO LEAVE

To what extent are you currently looking for a different job than the one you have now? Are you actively looking for another job, watching for opportunities but not actively looking, or are you not looking for another job?

% WATCHING FOR OR ACTIVELY SEEKING NEW JOB

Regional

47%

Global

51%

Gender

46% Female

48% Male

Age

56% <40 years old

40% ≥40 years old

Job Level

44% Manager

48% Individual contributor

Work Location

48% Exclusively remote

50% Hybrid

47% On-site

According to the survey, very nearly half of the employees in the workforce are watching for or actively seeking a new job, which is roughly consistent with some of the data we saw earlier on employee anger.

I suppose it is possible to be engaged and still be angry, but it's more likely that the people in the workforce that experience feelings of anger fall mostly in the "actively disengaged" group.

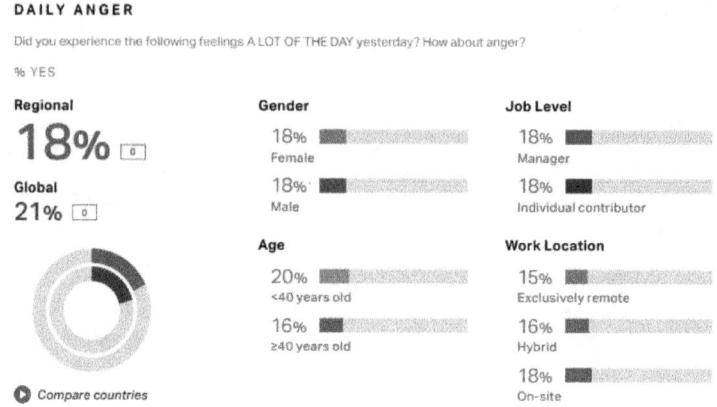

DAILY ANGER

Did you experience the following feelings A LOT OF THE DAY yesterday? How about anger?

% YES

Regional	Gender	Job Level
18%	18% Female	18% Manager
Global	18% Male	18% Individual contributor
21%		
	Age	**Work Location**
	20% <40 years old	15% Exclusively remote
	16% ≥40 years old	16% Hybrid
▶ Compare countries		18% On-site

Working Remotely and/or Hybrid Work

We all know that during Covid, there was a paradigm shift in some jobs and companies regarding showing up to the office.

The "hybrid" setup has been adopted by a lot of companies as a compromise plan.

The employees that have "hybrid" work are 7% more likely to be engaged than people who actually showed up at the office.

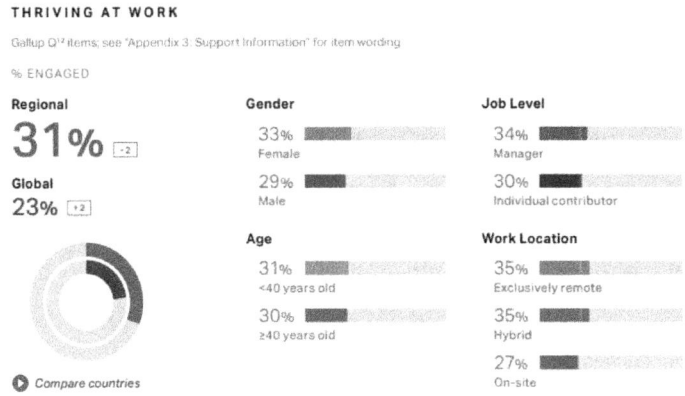

THRIVING AT WORK

Gallup Q¹² items; see "Appendix 3: Support Information" for item wording

% ENGAGED

Regional	Gender	Job Level
31% ⌐·²⌐	33% Female	34% Manager
Global	29% Male	30% Individual contributor
23% ⌐·²⌐	Age	Work Location
▶ Compare countries	31% <40 years old	35% Exclusively remote
	30% ≥40 years old	35% Hybrid
		27% On-site

Causes for Employee Disengagement

There are plenty of theories for this phenomenon. The article linked from XL-net has a list of 20 of these as follows:

Little purpose, meaning or connection

Stagnation

Poor Management

Lack of Communication

Lack of feedback

Inadequate Pay

Lack of Recognition

Poor Leadership

Minimal Training and Development

Excessive Workload

Minimal Tools and Resources

94

Limited Teamwork and Collaboration

Under or Over Qualification

Apathy

Personal and Workplace Challenges

Lack of Flexibility

Minimal Power or Autonomy

Lack of Respect

Poorly followed Values

The Effects of Employee Disengagement

Globally the Gallup Organization believes that employee disengagement costs the economy 9% of GDP, which is pretty consistent with what is going on globally.

That's about $8 trillion, which would be another California plus Texas plus New York if we, as a society could harness it.

There is an interesting moment in the video below from Ira Wolfe:

Hybrid Working Video Ira Woolfe

https://www.youtube.com/watch?v=EulgfRo5yNc

This states that the amount of customer engagement is roughly the same as the employee engagement, and the pre-and post- Covid shift in this measurement was very similar to one another.

This is about 31:40 of this interview with Gallup's Vibhas Ratanjee.

It goes on to say that there is a significant positive business outcome in organizations with high levels of employee engagement, which has been consistently measured for 28 years.

Employee Turnover

It's expensive to hire a new employee. If you are the manager of an "average" operation, and you're looking at a 50% disengagement rate, and only half of them go through with it, it'll result in significant expense just in terms of recruiting new employees. The article I've referenced says it's between $4000 and $20,000, depending on the employee.

Also, you are going to be in a situation where a significant portion of the workforce is "new" and that's bad for quality and customer satisfaction.

And, to make things much worse, which ones of your employees are going to leave? Is it the lazy, decadent, undertrained, ticked off and helpless ones? No, those are the ones that are going to stay. The employees that are going to leave are the aggressive self-starters and they're going to take co-workers with them.

You, as a manager, are aware of this, or if you weren't before, you are now. Half of your employees are on the verge of quitting. A reference earlier said that something on the order of 38% have actively quit within the last 18 months.

There are Many Questions

The first question is, why was this allowed to happen? The answer, unfortunately, 51% of managers are just as disengaged, and only 35% are actually engaged in their jobs, which is only marginally higher than the actual employees.

If you have a significant portion of the management of a place just as disengaged as the employees, how is this allowed to happen? That, of course is one of the four definitions of "Entrenched Mediocrity." An unacceptable condition is allowed to continue, to avoid the cost of change.

What would Fix It?

Aside from selecting "better" managers, as we have referenced previously, there are a number of suggested courses of action:

I suggest avoiding naming an "employee of the month" because an already ticked off workforce is going to dislike that.

I would say some of the better ideas are as follows:

Have a clearly defined company mission. I can't tell you how many companies I have been to where there is lack of clarity as to what the mission of the company is. Employees like for the work they are doing to be meaningful to society. Top management, whoever that is, also must live by the company values. There's nothing worse than a hypocritical boss that spouts the values on one day, and ignores it the next.

Provide some kind of training. One of the Lessons from Dog Training was that training makes you like the dog better, and the dog to like you better. This has been known to work for humans as well.

Recognize and reward employees. Warning: If the same employee wins Employee of the Month every month, it will be a demotivator.

Try to develop open communication and feedback. Employees should feel free to come up with suggestions for process improvements and constructively contribute to the business.

Promote healthy work habits. These may include flexible scheduling, ensuring a suitable space for employees to work

Encourage employee health. That also includes physical and mental health.

Promote team activities, including charity projects and other projects out of the office that make a difference to peoples' lives.

Encourage collaboration. Ask team members to address problems in the organization, and come up with solutions

Make sure employees have the right tools to do their jobs. There is nothing more unmotivating than a workplace that is not properly equipped.

Evaluate processes and introduce efficiencies. Employees can tell if they're being made to jump through a lot of hoops unnecessarily.

Assign employees to the right role

A chapter later will discuss the issue of employee "fit'"

Conduct surveys.

This is almost like the old-fashioned suggestion box, and one may only look at classic Simpsons episodes to see the humor in that.

Have a measurement of employee sentiment that is easy to track, and will alert the management if something changes. The best example of this I ever saw was in a place that made something very dangerous. The company had three buckets mounted in the main entry way, with a smiley, frowny and one in between. The employees were asked to throw a poker chip into whichever bucket they wanted when they walked through the gate. It was not scientific except to say that the plant management could tell if something was changing, such as excessive overtime or other workplace condition, and potentially do something about it before large numbers of workers got ticked off.

Movie References

For further viewing, I happen to like the following two movies:

Office Space (1999)

Office Space Trailer

https://youtu.be/3_fG_zLbBeU?si=zZfrqrKoVRWonsUi

A disengaged group of employees, faced with useless tasks in a sterile office environment go over to the dark side and take matters into their own hands.

Spoiler alert, the Swingline company had to come up with a red stapler in response to this film.

Employee of the Month (2006)

Employee Of The Month trailer

https://youtu.be/v8HrbXohzX8?si=EszloOe1Pm-bAp7y

A disengaged, wrongly placed, unmotivated employee in a retail operation finds additional motivation to challenge the entrenched, mediocre, obnoxious team "alpha."

Feel free to suggest your own.

Is it Natural to Hate Your Work?

I've linked an article from Psychology Today that raises this question. It suggests that the above concept of "engagement" only works for the top ½ of the workforce.

The bottom 60% of the workforce has had a net inflation-adjusted decrease in median income since 1974. For those workers, particularly the ones at the bottom who are put into dirty, dangerous jobs, and limited to less-than-full-time hours are not going to spend too much time worrying about employee engagement.

For this workforce, there is a situation of not having their basic needs met. Of course, they're not engaged in their work.

There is also an article linked from the Institute for Health Incentives that says boredom at work is your brain's way of alerting you that you are in a potentially unhealthy situation.

What to make of all of this?

In our journey to try to figure out why people don't do their jobs, we've already learned a lot. A drunk, disengaged, ticked off, unprepared workforce, using obsolete equipment, and managed by ineffective managers that got their job for wearing a nice suit in the office are expected to do some tasks.

We've also found out that the typical employee gets less training than the family dog.

We also know that due to Entrenched Mediocrity, changing any of this is nearly impossible. This is, assuming there is some awareness on the part of management. There are often underlying reasons for this, including, but not limited to, the manager is the boss's decadent nephew, or the jerk line manager is the boss's original employee who was fine as a gofer, but terrible as a manager.

Is it any wonder that it is a golden age for people like me who profit off of this stuff?

Links and References

08 Mccaig's Law

This is the story of Mccaig's Law.

Mccaig was a short, mouthy Canadian, from a little mining town clear up north. He had been a minor league hockey player. I am not going to tell you the whole story. That's for someone else to tell.

But what I am going to say is that he was a "character." It is possible that he is still around. He was in his mid-50's at the time I knew him 30 years ago. He was also a magnificent bullshit artist that found himself as the facilities manager over a scientific laboratory. The technicians were bright, but cooped up, and like all bright, cooped up people in a work group, there were always a lot of little petty conflicts and politics going on, and often, he was in the middle of it.

Anyway, at one point he told me something I never forgot. He said "Jim, if you want to see how a place is being run, go into the employees' restroom, and see how nasty it is. If it's nice, it shows that the company is well run."

Public Restrooms

I've spent a lot of time, over the last 30 years, validating Mccaig's law, and particularly in the last 10 when I've audited the quality systems in major corporations and "world class" operations, and I believe it to be true.

Restrooms are a commitment.

When you install one in the first place, you're first proving that you understand human frailty. The need to use the restroom is universal. But once you've installed it, it's a public symbol of your commitment to human respect and to maintain it in an orderly fashion.

The essence of McCaig's law is that it is a measurement of the management's commitment to anything. If you let that slide, what else are you letting slide?

Nothing Happens in Isolation

This quote is attributed to David McCullough. It basically states that everything constructed by humans, including political systems, institutions, and everything else, is interconnected.

This theory is applied equally to homeless animals. If you live in a place with a lot of homeless and abandoned animals, it's a barometer of what's going on in a place.

If you want to think of a rest room as the equivalent of a stray dog, you'd be pretty close to correct.

Rest Room Niceness

So, what does it take to maintain a nice restroom? Well, to make a long story short, you, as an organization, have to try.

You, the management, must prioritize it, along with a lot of the other things in your place. You must provide resources for it, including its periodic refurbishment. You need to design it in the first place, do maintenance, monitor its condition, and pay someone to clean it.

But before any of these other things, you have to try. You, the boss, must walk in the door in the morning and say, "You know what? not everything will go my way today, but the thing under my control, namely the restroom, will be nice."

https://youtu.be/YHwOtVqgVDQ

Rest Room Organization

In most of the places I go, there is a boss. Or to be perfectly specific, there may be a management team.

Part of the management activity is facility management. This may or may not be the same as plant maintenance. Depending on the size and complexity of the company, there may be a separate infrastructure department, that maintains the restrooms, along with providing insect control and changing burned out light bulbs.

Side rant: While we're on the topic of light bulbs, that's another stray dog of a thing that is often missed. What's especially annoying is a burned-out bulb on one of these big old control panels with the flashing lights.

A lot of these have been replaced by digital control systems that give you information on your process in real time on some kind of computer screen.

But some of them, not so much.

I used to have a job in a place that ran a reactor that was very dangerous, and very hot. At the top of this thing was an after burner that burned off all the noxious gases that were generated by the process. This thing had a control panel, and the control panel had lights. These lights gave you information, such as whether the thing was going to imminently blow up.

The maintenance guy in this place was entrenched and mediocre. He did only enough work to keep the place running poorly, but because he had been around long enough to know where all the skeletons were buried, the boss, who was a bit insecure, didn't want to fire him.

On most of these instrument panels there is a test button. If you push it, it'll light up all the lights on the panel board so you can tell if any of them are burned out. On this thing, about half of them were burned out, including the one that says, "too hot."

So, I asked this guy about it, and his response was "Aw, that light don't mean nothin.'"

But my statement was "yes it does, it means the maintenance department is lazy. It tolerates a safety condition in a dangerous piece of equipment and refuses to change a simple light bulb."

The restrooms in the production part of that place were nasty, but in the office, where the boss sat, they were more tolerable. That happens a lot too. What message does that send to the production workers?

The Low Wage Worker

There is a facility manager, but he or she hardly ever cleans the rest room personally. They either have a janitorial staff that does this job, or more often nowadays, there is a janitorial subcontractor.

The actual human that does this job is a low wage worker, very often female, very often just hired off the street. Welcome to Enviro-temp Corp, the restroom subcontractor. Here's your cleaning stuff, go clean this restroom. There is a subcontractor supervisor that usually hands them the mop and bucket.

It's very likely that this person will do a half-assed job.

So that's the organization. Boss, facility manager, subcontractor boss, and then low wage worker. The last two people in the chain have no ownership of the place. They won't even use the restroom themselves, and they're gone once they've cleaned it. A lot of times, this happens at night when no one is supervising them at all. That's the very definition of disengagement.

So, it would not be surprising at all if some of these restrooms, over a period, become funky. Restrooms are not unique that way. Most pieces of equipment that process "biomatter" tend to build up funk over time, if you don't clean them thoroughly. The people that process drugs and food know this very well. They have methods to detect bacteria on production equipment, and track this. These places know how to clean things, and in a general way, the restrooms in these places are reasonable for that reason.

The same can be said for the floor, countertops and other surfaces. The food people control this stuff very well.

Truck stops do not control this very well. Except "Buc-Ees." Those restrooms are magnificent.

The Alarm Systems and Feedback Processes
So, you have a restroom, and you don't want it to get funky. You do want to keep it orderly and make sure all the fixtures are running properly.

You need some sort of inspection process and/or system by which the facility manager can be alerted to the condition if it becomes nasty. Ideally, the facility manager can and should be checking the restrooms him or herself, and taking personal responsibility, but that doesn't always happen. Ideally, the janitorial resource should notice it themselves, and fix it without being told.

But that rarely happens. This is where it almost gets funny, from a quality systems standpoint. How many times have you been in a restroom, and on the back of the door, there's a checklist that says "yeah, I, the assigned worker inspected the place and found it to be OK?"

I should probably do a separate chapter on checklists.

The thing about a restroom checklist: Are there company standards on what a properly cleaned restroom should look like? And, if so, does a new employee, or subcontractor, get

109

training on this topic? If not, how do you know the employee didn't stick his or her head in the door, say "yeah, it's good" and check the box?

One person's clean restroom is not quite like another's.

What exactly does it tell you when the box hasn't been checked in a couple of weeks? It tells you that both the cleaner and the boss aren't paying attention because everybody in the place can see what happened, including the customers. Maybe the cleaner has walked off the job, and they haven't gotten around to replacing him or her. That sends another message.

I will have much more to say about alarms and feedback processes later. Once the condition is noticed, what's the plan and urgency about fixing it?

General Observations

I can't give you any more history, examples, or other information than the Toilet Guru can. He is linked in the links and references.

The most beautiful restroom in Atlanta is at the Crown Plaza Ravinia, not far from the conference room. Why? It's attached to the world headquarters of IHG group, which is the company that runs the Holiday Inn, and all the big shots walk around it.

The Home Depot, Ingles Grocery Stores, and Chick Fil A typically do a good job on their public toilets.

The most beautiful industrial toilet I have been to is in a place that was owned by Procter and Gamble. This is the company that makes all the cleaning products, paper products and the like, that are used for this job. I was particularly impressed by the cushy toilet paper and paper towels at that place.

Germany and Japan, overall, don't spend too much time on this topic. Their loss. I was in an Italian rest room one time that was so beautiful I was hesitant to soil it. That's who they are, I guess. The toilets in Malaysia, which is 60% Muslim, accommodate the need for this culture to clean themselves left-handed. You can get details on this elsewhere.

I was in a bathroom in Japan one time that looked like it was cleaned robotically. To the extent I could tell, there were high pressure nozzles in the wall everywhere that occasionally blasted the place, like an automatic car wash. I am not completely sure how they kept people out of it when that was happening.

Places where the employees vandalize the restrooms? That's a red flag. South America is rough. I never made it to Africa, but I heard it was also rough. The toilets in New Zealand don't flush counterclockwise. They're made to use little, or no water and they sort of tumble vertically. Maybe that says a lot about them.

Why is any of this important?

A restroom, as McCaig pointed out, is the result and artifact of a complex system of design, implementation, and resource allocation as it applies to maintenance.

People that are good at things tend to be good at several things. The same can be said about people that are crappy about things.

So, think about McCaig's Law going forward as we explore why people don't do their jobs, and give this some thought to the complex system the next time you visit a restroom, including your own.

Links and References

Why People Don't Do Their Jobs

09 Entrenched Mediocrity

Entrenched Mediocrity is the answer to the "next question." We talked in the introduction about the "five why" method of root cause analysis. This book was written because of the idea that people do a lot of analysis and come up with "human error" as the solution. But accepting that, they still do not fix the problem.

Or, to put it a different way, you know there's a problem, you know the solution, why didn't you fix it?

There are the four working definitions of "Entrenched Mediocrity."

An obvious beneficial change is resisted, especially for non-technical reasons

The organization accepts mediocrity to avoid the cost of change

A widely known problem is allowed to continue despite obvious risk

Overhead activities become more important than production

A given organizational issue can have elements of more than one of these definitions. In fact, that case is the more common.

More About Mediocrity
We know all about mediocrity. It's being passable, it's being "adequate" it's being "ordinary."

114

There is plenty in the literature about being ordinary and hating it, but a lot of people, organizations and nations are ordinary and like it that way.

It's not necessarily evil, but it is a loss of human potential. Also, as we're about to see, it's temporary.

We also know about being entrenched. This is about a sufficiently established, well-established, and deep-rooted condition. Often it is human, but it doesn't have to be. It isn't "immovable" per se. With some amount of effort, a well-established piece of concrete can be blasted out. But there is often a significant effort involved.

That being the case, there are four specific definitions for Entrenched Mediocrity

Change Resistance for Non-Technical Reasons

I have an example of this in this little video that I did a few years ago:

https://youtu.be/Lc9a-J2RmhQ

I didn't do my job of checking a box, because the box scrolled off the top of my screen when I uploaded a few documents. It wasn't just me. This was a common failure mode, and a lot of people in the organization I was in were doing the same thing.

That would make it a systemic problem.

So, a systemic problem usually requires that some system be changed to solve it. But in this case, a big organization, it was utterly impossible to get that level of change done, even though the creation of an error trap or other method is fast and easy.

The organization may have its reasons for not making the change. This is IT related, and IT activities are notorious for this. The IT department is typically overworked, and in a lot of places it is work like resetting peoples' passwords and hand holding, and once the change is made, they must be able to roll it out to X number of thousands of remote viewers. The software itself was developed "pre-cloud" thus making it a "legacy system."

To make a long story short, the immediate short-term solution was determined to be "beat on the victim" rather than solve the problem.

Avoiding the Cost of Change

In this definition, mediocrity is accepted to avoid the cost of change. I believe we can all think of examples of this in our personal and work lives.

If you want an example, you can look at the famous episode of the GM vehicles whose ignition switch shut off while driving, particularly if the driver had a lot of heavy stuff attached to the key ring.

The problem was known for a long time, and attributed to a cheap plastic part, the cost of which was estimated by Time Magazine as less than $1 per car.

The cost to fix the ignition switches was estimated to be about $350 per car.

The problem was known for about a decade before anything was done about it, and the company accepted the risk to avoid the cost of re-engineering the part, which could have been done cheaply.

Car recalls happen all the time. We will look at another example later, but to make a long story short, the company accepted a part that worked in a mediocre fashion to avoid the cost of changing it. A further argument is that they knew the risk and accepted it. We're going to talk about that later, but it is very common.

The Leaning Toilet

In an organization, if this type of mediocrity happens too often, it becomes a possible source of workplace toxicity. To use a toilet example: A place where I once worked had a terrible rest room situation. There was a work group of about 20 people, and the toilet was terrible. By this I mean that it wobbled annoyingly anytime anyone sat on it.

Because of the workforce's gender composition, this was considered less of a problem. With a 20-man work group, it was only sat on a few times per day, even though it was "used" more than that. Anyone who did sit on it ran the risk of it tipping over, which ticked off anyone who did so to the extent that it affected their overall office experience. This was a time and place that didn't care too much about the office experience.

One sunny day, this toilet tipped over, with someone sitting on it. This was regarded at the time as funny, because it was the cranky old lab manager, and it became a bit of an inside joke. But as the marketing people say, this was something we call a "pain point." A symbol to the universe that the company was too cheap to take care of its employees.

And, consistent with McCaig's Law, this idea also carried through to other parts of the operation.

Risk Acceptance

There is an element of risk acceptance in a lot of these examples.

In this definition, a widely known problem is allowed to continue despite obvious risk. There doesn't have to be cost, or anyone's feelings involved, but there can be.

Here's my favorite example.

I was given the opportunity at one point to improve the profitability of a little processing operation. In this operation, there was a big propane furnace, a process input which was a bit annoying, and a process output which was also a bit annoying but less so.

The furnace itself was developed by a fellow who I knew personally. He lived out the dream that some of us have of inventing something and then turning it into a commercially successful venture. At one point, he hired a "gofer" who worked beside him to learn the process.

At some later point, the process was sold to an Angel Investor, and the founder retired. Gofer was hired to be the plant manager, since he knew how to run the process. At about that time, a second plant, also founded by the inventor, blew up and killed a lot of people. So, it was recognized that the process itself was dangerous, and you had to know what the hell you were doing to run it.

The Plot Thickens

So, my job in this was, as an employee of the angel investor, to go in, get information about how to run the system, and if possible, make improvements. A side complication was that this place was about 300 miles away, and the idea was hatched of the possibility of moving it.

The Gofer/plant manager was big, profane and rude, and at one point threatened me with physical violence. Since he was also well known to be carrying firearms, I did what I could to get some information, and reported it back to the organization. Come to find out that he was doing the same thing to everybody, even the owners of the company.

After I did a few calculations, I found out that the process itself was about 2% thermodynamically efficient based on the amount of propane used and the heat generated, 98% of the fuel cost was going up the stack as waste heat.

Not long after that, the UPS driver that went to that place reported to the company the suspicion that the employee was selling and using illegal drugs out of the plant. Heaven is High, and the emperor is Far Away, as the saying goes.

So, the obvious risks were: Only one person knew how to "safety" run a dangerous process. That person was also at risk of being busted for drug sales, and probable use.

I have been in similar situations several times over the years, and the most professionally run organizations fire everybody involved, and if need be close the place down. This organization chose to accept both risks and continue to operate at 2% efficiency. There was a cost consideration, and the consideration of the cost of walking away.

I will let you be the judge of what should have been done, but I believe this sort of thing happens all the time. Everything was fine yesterday, so we'll let it run and hope the situation lasts for another day.

Overhead Activities

The last of these definitions involves overhead activities. Overhead activities are prioritized over production.

I have a funny video on this, too:

https://youtu.be/rd3Ygnb__TA

The Roman Empire took 900 years to build, and 80 years to destroy. I will let you study the causes of the collapse of the Roman Empire, but I think it was this: The population was too preoccupied with bureaucracy, religion, and sporting events to realize that an army carrying spears and rocks was about to sack it.

I will let you do further research on the character Tom Peters, who did a lot of work back in the 1980's on "excellence."

He tells the story of Nucor Steel, who back in the 1980's was one of the pioneers of the strategy of small and agile, and capturing small markets. The idea they had was "flattening the layers" in that there were only four levels of organization between the CEO and the plant floor. To accomplish that, there had to be a conscious management decision to limit the size of the manufacturing facilities.

In my opinion, as someone who has been in more than a hundred companies, including startups and huge corporations and every place between, there are two critical times in the development of an organization.

Lessons from Startups

One is when the organization reaches about 15 people. That's roughly the number of people that an entrepreneur can boss around in one day. Any more than that makes it too hard for one person to monitor. Above that number,

121

the boss must develop and implement processes and procedures, and that isn't easy. It requires a different skillset from the one that started the company in the first place.

Another is when they reach about 100 people. The above fellow from Nucor, Ken Iverson, identified that number as the point at which people stop talking to each other. The communication processes become too complicated, and problem solving becomes more difficult.

It's also the point at which someone can make a career out of saying "no." I worked for a place for a while in which about ⅓ of the technical management of the place literally built a career out of rejecting research and development activities.

I will let you figure out how this works in the work organizations you are involved in, but to make a long story short, if an organization gets to be so big and so old that it is easy to kill an opportunity, that's not good.

Ken Iverson himself passed away in 2002. According to the article which I have linked in the links and references, The organizational structure is still flat and decentralized. Their earnings have gone from about $200 million, since 2002, to $9.7 Billion today, and earnings per ton from $42 to $400 in that time.

Resistance

The writer Stephen Pressfield has come up with the concept of Resistance, which we will talk about later.

Resistance is defined as the universal force that keeps things the same. He sees this in his context as a writer. Resistance is the force that keeps writers from writing, painters from painting, and organizations from organizing. It accepts people living in a van down by the river.

But as he points out, it only works in one direction. Resistance keeps people and organizations and nations from getting to a higher form of existence. But it does not keep them from getting worse. There is a universal force, entropy, that will pull you, your organization, and your society downward if you let it.

So that's the danger of Entrenched Mediocrity. At some point, it leads to organizational decline and collapse, if it is permitted to continue.

Maybe that's why I am writing this. My contribution to the enhancement of humankind. I'm trying to keep that from happening.

Entrenched Mediocrity
Here is your project: As we go through some of these examples, of "why people don't do their jobs" and why some of these things happened, think of them all as some artifact of the four types of 'entrenched mediocrity."

It won't necessarily help anyone change it, but at least you'll understand that mediocrity is also endemic to the human condition and is very difficult to overcome.

Links and References

10 Lessons from Dog Training

We're going to talk about training now, and how training people is similar enough to dog training. After having trained a dog, to tell the honest truth, it's easier than training a human.

The reason we're focused on this now is that lack of training is a key excuse why people don't do their jobs. I know this is that in my work in quality systems auditing, I've probably seen documentation of several hundred quality incidents a year, and "lack of training" in a factory screwup situation is the most common answer. Someone is brought in, put on the job without either understanding it or without developing dexterity, and the work doesn't get done properly.

You don't have to be in manufacturing to see examples of this. I searched for "golf training" and got 429 million hits, which is not as many as "my boss is an idiot" but still a significant number.

We all know that because of turnover in the workplace, about one third of the workforce is new in their jobs. 23% of the US workforce quit in 2021, and 38 million people quit in 2022, and they were all replaced by the "new guy." No wonder the systems are starting to break down. The current adjusted "quit rate" from the BLS as of mid-2023 is about 2.9% per month, although I suppose some of these people quit more than once.

Resistance to Employee Training

There are some articles in the Links and References on this topic. Come to find out, according to the survey, 59% of the workforce didn't get training, and they essentially learned their jobs themselves, and only 29% of employees are satisfied with their level of training.

There are several reasons that employers don't want to train people. Numbers one and two are that it takes time and costs money. Evidently the most popular solution to the problem of training is to just send someone out onto the floor without it and let them figure it out.

According to an article linked from Zippia, 92% of employees say that training activities have a positive effect on their "engagement" when "properly planned." And companies with comprehensive training programs have a 24% higher profit margin than the non-trainers.

So, we're in a situation of divergence where employers dislike paying money to train people at the very same time, they're having to do more of it. At the same time, activities like customer service, where people are sick of talking to people who don't know anything and give them wrong advice, is seen as important by 97% of customers.

Examples of Badly Trained Workers

We don't have to work too hard to find people who don't know what they are doing. Let me give you an example. I was working in a place that processes PVC. That's polyvinyl chloride, aka plastic, that is used in all sorts of applications.

The number one cause of defects in the finished product in this place was contamination. I knew this but it evidently wasn't common knowledge among the actual employees. I was being shown around by the production manager.

We got to a big, noisy piece of equipment where these big blobs of hot plastic were coming out, and then sheeted off to go downstream to be molded into something.

A fellow was pulling them out of the machine, and throwing them onto the floor, which was dirty, and to get them to spread out he was walking around on them, with shoes that were dirty.

So, I said to the production manager, who was new: "Wait a minute. You mean to say that you let these guys walk around on the material?" He replied "Uh, yeah, that's a new guy, he just came in off the street. You can't expect him to know everything." I made a face and moved on.

There are four problems in a nutshell. The job itself wasn't well enough understood by whoever was doing the training. The employee wasn't trained to do his job properly. Feedback from the system that said contamination was an issue wasn't getting to the employee, and the production manager had sympathy for the worker and didn't put a stop to it.

I see this stuff all the time. I have stories, because in complex organizations, you can't train common sense.

Lessons from Dog Training

According to the American Kennel Club, 73% of dog owners are now doing dog training, and since Covid, spending on training methods and devices has surged.

What that means is that people are now more willing to train their dogs than their employees.

Reasons for training your dog are as follows;

Your dog won't poop on the floor or chew furniture (unwanted behavior)

It's better for the dog to be intellectually and physically stimulated

The dog is less likely to run away and get hit by a car

You like the dog better

Dog likes you better

It builds the dog's confidence.

Dog less likely to bite the neighbor

Neighbor less likely to hate you and the dog

Reasons for training your workforce are as follows:

Improved employee skills

Increased productivity

Faster ramp times

Higher job satisfaction

Lower turnover

Improved buyer experience

Increased consistency

Enhanced customer relationships

They're basically the same reasons. Less unwanted behavior, fewer problems, and improved "production", whatever that is. Plus, your employees won't bite the neighbors.

Cesar Millan

According to sources, the current most famous dog trainer in the world is Cesar Milan, aka "the Dog Whisperer" from TV.

He grew up on a farm in Mexico and learned his "dog training methods" from his mother. He arrived in the US at some point and made his reputation by walking packs of up to 40 dogs around some of the roughest areas of Los Angeles. He founded the "Dog Psychology Center" in 2008, after he figured out there was a market for getting dogs away from their overindulgent owners and training them to be like animals. He hit "rock bottom" in 2010, heavily in debt and attempting suicide.

The TV show ran from 2004 through 2012, making this fellow a household name, based on his connection with problem dogs.

At the same time all of this was going on, the show received criticism from the "animal behavior community" because he refused to put up with BS from dogs and treated them in a doglike farm-dog manner, as humans have done throughout history.

Here's a video:

Cesar Millan Video

https://www.youtube.com/watch?v=--8ItQos-lc

Millan's method sees the connection between the dog behavior and the human that tolerates and sometimes encourages the behavior. He teaches his students, who are humans, to read the signs of dog behavior and act accordingly. This particularly includes the fraction of dogs with personality disorders and anxiety, which are known to be problematic.

He currently has a show "Better Humans Better Dogs" which emphasizes this point. For somewhere between $50K and $100K you, too, can have Cesar come to your business event and give "Motivational Training" to your workforce.

Frank Inn

Frank Inn (1916-2002) trained numerous animals for film and TV, including "Cat" from Breakfast at Tiffany's, "Arnold Ziffel" the trained pig(s) from Green Acres, and a brown mutt named "Higgins" who became more famous as the TV and movie dog "Benji." He was assistant to Frank Weatherwax, the trainer who trained "Toto" on "The Wizard of Oz." and several of the "Rin Tin Tins".

He taught "his way" to a lot of assistants, who are now carrying on his traditions.

He was able to get these animals to do intricate tricks by establishing a connection with them. This connection was so close that he maintained a collection of their cremated remains throughout his place in Beverly Hills. Reportedly, they couldn't bury the remains of the four "Arnolds" with him according to regulations.

He pioneered the training method of not holding his trainees down by the neck while they freaked out and bit him, which is Cesar's method.

Frank Inn Video

https://www.youtube.com/watch?v=7jmINs1TkJE

The method for training a pig is straightforward, according to the American Mini Pig association, they're highly motivated by food, thrive on routine, and won't cooperate when they're hungry.

There's a link in the links and references, which you can refer to when you're ready to do your next training session.

The trick, as it were, to training many different species is that no two trainees are alike, the reward system is different, and you can't nag them, because you don't know their language.

BF Skinner

BF Skinner (2004-1990) was the father of something called "Operant Conditioning." Here is how it works: You take an animal (he preferred a bird) and starve it down to some fraction of its normal body weight. Then, you teach it to press a little lever which releases a little food.

Pretty soon the animal figures it out and will start pressing the lever.

This method later was modified by adding a second lever to give a little shock to the animal if they screwed up. The combination of starvation, rewards and shocks lead most animals to be trained to do a job fairly quickly.

But you can't really do this method with people, and in this period, you can't really do it with animals either.

Furthermore, if you have more than one lever, and randomize the pain and reward so that the animal can't form any patterns, the animal will crawl into a corner and be traumatized. It only works if you're consistent.

This whole area is a giant can of worms that includes various topics in psychology, and I am not authoritative to write about it other than to refer you somewhere.

The "Training Humans" podcast is an entertaining way to be reminded of this can of worms, which includes manipulation, deceitfulness, cult leaders, drug dealers and the like. The main lesson on this is that you must be very careful of what you consider "desirable behavior" and not unintentionally discourage it by making the punishment. unclear.

Imitation Learning

This is probably the most frequent type of workplace learning now. It basically says "Hello, new person, this is Joe. Go out and do what he does, and after you've done this, you'll be considered "trained.""

In other words, this is "on the job training."

This type of training is very popular for several reasons: It has the advantage that you can expose the employee to real situations and gets employees "up to speed" reasonably quickly. Also, you can use this to test employee attributes such as decision making and dexterity. It allows you to get "work" out of someone just off the street, and in a sense, builds some teamwork.

Here are your problems: First, it's the laziest possible form of training for management, because it absolves them from understanding the job. Secondly, Joe himself might be threatened by a new employee who he correctly sees as someone who might take his job. Thirdly, it's only as good as Joe and unless someone refreshes "Joe's" training occasionally, there could be some bad habits incorporated in the "training" that you'd prefer not to reinforce.

It in essence is one degree of separation away from "throwing someone to the wolves" with all its associated safety, quality, financial and institutional risk.

Experience vs. Training

I do some work with several companies that outsource Internet Security activities. They are recruiters and hire this type of employee for clients and the government. In that industry, there is a certification process, and most of the time the people that get the big bucks are highly experienced in the field.

So, when the client finally puts them in the job, they already have a high level of knowledge about the protocols and methods, and they don't need training, other than "here is your badge to get in the front door, the bathroom is down the hall to the left. Here's your computer, read this security training and get to work."

What I am saying is that in some cases, employers are willing to pay a premium for experienced workers that they can put into a job right away.

But the training idea depends highly on how much respect "the management" gives to the job. In that case it's a small world and the experts in it know each other.

Training Advice

If you use your search engine and enter "training advice for dogs" you get 116 million results. If you search "training advice for employees" you get 1.2 billion, which flies in the face of the statistic above that says people are more likely to train a dog than an employee.

All I can give you is some key points which are common to most of these. All of these are predicated on basic socialization and correctly selecting the right dog for the job.

Establish a connection between the trainer and the trainee. This is hard if there are language/culture/personality issues.

Drive fear out of the system

Individualize the training program. No two trainees are alike or learn the same.

Deconstruct the task so both trainer and trainee can understand it

Balance repetition with variation so the trainer and trainee maintain engagement

Offer a reward. Not every trainee values the same reward.

Don't quit too early. Train until you achieve the desired behavior.

End on a positive note.

https://youtu.be/5DZ1f6YbNIs

https://youtu.be/MUNa_NnjqIg

My Training Story

When I started my first job out of college, "they" basically said "congratulations for graduating from college. Now forget all of that and we will train you about how we do things."

The job itself was sort of a process engineering job, where I went out into a vast manufacturing plant with flashing lights and forklifts. I was supposed to do process measurements and help make quality-related decisions and disposition defective materials.

There was supposed to be a two-week training course in each of three areas of the plant I was working in, one of which was the analytical lab. When they found out that I knew what I was doing "They" told me to stay in there for a couple of months to allow them to be caught up while the lab people were on vacation.

At some point "they" decided "screw all that, let's throw him to the wolves." I shadowed a senior employee for a couple of weeks, and then was assigned an area of the plant. After about three months of that I was put on the evening shift, which was fine. Other than a few temperature readings, the rest was reactive. The supervisor or shift foreman would call me and I'd have to go out and help him or her solve a problem, despite three months on the job. My main function was communication of quality issues back to the higher-level management who then either reacted or not.

In theory I was supposed to advise supervisors with 30 years of experience in the nuances of their job. No wonder there was hostility. Everything was adversarial. I'll write a book about that later. There were a lot of "human skills" involved. If you were particularly crappy at those, you had a lot of problems.

Within a year or two I was adding value and was able to make some multiple hundred-thousand-dollar process adjustments that helped productivity. I also got good at getting rid of defective material by either making formula adjustments or blending in a controlled way, and that got me some respect from some of the management.

Why there was defective material in the first place is one of the sources of this book. It boils down to entrenched mediocrity. There was a piece of equipment in the plant that was bought by the company founder in 1910.

Was the "training" effective? Well, some of it stayed with me to today, so I guess you would say so. I guess you couldn't have done that with most people off the street, as I now know.

What would have worked better?

I think paid internships would have been much better. I would have had a much better idea of the functioning of the place, while I was still in college. I'd have been exposed to work-life, the "throwing to the wolves" wouldn't have been a shock to the plant employees, and it would have been better.

But it would have been slower and from the point of view of the company they may have trained a lot of interns before they found a few that would stay. As it was, they were hiring people in my position about every three years, and there was no real career path after that. Their loss.

In this era a lot of colleges require an internship at some time during your college experience, which I believe is good, in technical fields like I was in.

People that Aren't Trainable

There is a certain fraction of the population that is not trainable. We talked about that a little bit earlier. Jordan Peterson, current internet talking head, has a lot to say about this:

Some People Can't be Trained

https://www.youtube.com/watch?v=fjs2gPa5sD0

There's no substitute for doing appropriate employee selection and matching people to their job from the standpoint of intelligence and social factors.

But as we will find out later, it's hard to correctly match people with jobs. It's equally bad to put a Top Gun Pilot, with super intelligence and dexterity into the wrong job as it is someone from the other end of the bell curve.

Links and References

11 Equipment Failure

We're going to talk about equipment failure now, which an important topic. Equipment failure is a common excuse given for people not doing their jobs. The press was down, so we couldn't do our jobs, or in IT, "the server was down so we couldn't do our jobs." We have all heard it.

The general rules for equipment maintenance, or equipment "reliability" differ slightly depending on whether a company is family-owned, publicly traded, a farm, which might or might not be family owned, or an IT situation where the "equipment" is a lot of servers and PCs.

It also has its ironic roots in McCaig's Law and Entrenched Mediocrity.

The Dividend Growth Model
Let's start with this.

The fundamental job of management is to increase the wealth of the shareholders. That means, in the publicly traded companies the job is to increase the stock price. This is so much of a thing that a lot of the management of the business has their salary based on this, and many are given stock as part of their compensation package so they have skin in the game.

The same is less true for family businesses, and even less true for family farms, whose main job is to provide income for the owners, and maybe have a solid business to pass down to the kids. In IT this might be truer.

So "growth" is a major component of this. You've heard the term "growth stock," those stocks are more valuable in the marketplace because the business is growing every year.

When these people purchase capital equipment, they know that a few years down the road they're going to need more capacity, because they expect the company to grow. One option is to buy more equipment when it is needed, and another option is to run the equipment faster so that you can produce more of whatever. In automotive you also have the insanity of the supply contracts requiring a lower selling price every year, meaning the need for improved efficiency every year is built into the business.

That's the basic problem. There will be constant pressure to run existing equipment faster and faster, because all of the incentives for management are to produce a growing amount of product at the lowest cost, and at the lowest capital expense possible. At the same time, the older the equipment gets, the worse it functions.

In a family business, this is basically the same because, in most cases, the owner is cheap. They also have competition from bigger and better competitors. On a farm this is not usually the case, what the farmer is mainly interested in is efficiency as long as their farms stay the same size. In the IT business there is an ongoing headwind of innovation, and expansion of data processing demand, because that is the way that business works. They need to constantly renew their equipment because if they don't they run the risk of having it be obsolete all at once and causing disruptions.

So, as we are saying, in most of the economy, there is a lot of incentive to buy your equipment as cheaply as possible, and run it into the ground or as hard as possible. What then happens is that "they" whine when something breaks down, when the primary cause of all of this is management decision making, and Entrenched Mediocrity. A known problem is allowed to continue despite obvious risk.

Maintenance vs. Reliability

What that also means is that the organization's attitude toward maintenance will differ depending on where they are in the economy, and their expectations about the future.

The average life span of an automotive plant is about 25 years. That means, on average, that the management has in the back of their minds that whatever equipment they install at startup will not be around forever.

What they really want is for that equipment to be reliable for that "foreseeable life." So, it is desirable to have what is called a "culture of reliability" which puts a lot of time and effort into maintaining the equipment for as long as that takes. But there is a cost associated with preventive maintenance, with the understanding that the equipment will wear out anyway.

https://youtu.be/56YY6JUXl5M

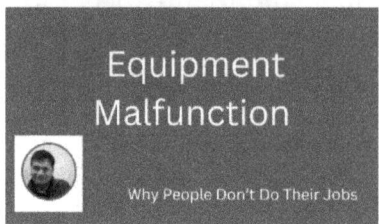

The average life span of a combine, the most expensive equipment on a farm, is 17 years, and it goes through 5 different owners. The average life span of a server in IT is 7-10 years but, in some cases, it is lower than that, 3-5 years.

Or the management can be mediocre and entrenched, and run everything into the ground, and toward the end of the life span, use emergency methods to keep the whole thing running. That's where the quality issues and people not doing their jobs come in.

Reasons for Equipment Failure

Okay then, after all that, here is a list of reasons for equipment failure, as posted by Farm Progress website.

145

Description	Comments
Not Reading the Operator's Manual	Ref: "Top Gun Pilots"
Improper Maintenance	The engineers who design and have experience with these things often put information in the operating manual, which is often second-guessed
Poor Electrical Connections ref: dirt and contamination	Dirty connectors are a primary reason for this, which means that someone didn't do the job of cleaning it.
Overrunning Machine Capacity	See above, this is an artifact of the Dividend Growth Model which says to milk every possible unit out of the equipment you can.
Not replacing worn parts	This is an organizational culture issue.
Misaligned tighteners	This is typical of farm equipment mainly, but there are tighteners on

	every car and fork lift.
Improper storage/shut down	Depending on the equipment shutdown protocol is a key to equipment life, especially in equipment which has a heat/cool cycle.
Weather-related issues	A lot of the responsible farmers of this age have metal buildings or other structures to keep their $250,000 combine from being snowed on.
Ignoring Warning Signals	Ref: Alarm Systems, people ignore flashing lights and weird sounds.
Untrained Operators	Ref: Temps and Doubtsourcing and the "new guy" being put on the machine without proper training.

The Failure Mode Commonalities

They're all human. These things, as a fundamental component, rely on people doing their jobs. They rely on a workforce that can read instructions, follow simple directions, react properly to flashing red lights, and in a general way, keep things running.

Therefore, they're subject to all of the systems we saw earlier about people not doing their jobs, in that if you as an organization don't have healthy systems to hire, train, motivate and otherwise engage a workforce that is capable of properly operating equipment and turning a wrench to fix it, the whole system, such as it is, will end up collapsing.

That goes double for IT nerds.

Other Considerations

There are a couple of other things to think about.

The first example of this is found in tools.

I have linked a video about this topic. If you take some indestructible Craftsman tools from the 50's and do functionality tests compared to today, typically, the old tools perform at the equivalent of today's high-end tools.

We haven't lost the technology to produce tough, versatile tools, but we've chosen to use cheap imported tools instead. I am as guilty as anybody. If I need a tool around the house, I am going to go to the cheap imported tool store and buy one that will work for the job at hand.

But what that also reflects is changes in metallurgy, corrosion resistance, vibration control, and fatigue which have led to an overall cheapening of things. That is a market decision that has been made by "the marketplace" in that the tools we have will do the job, temporarily, and since people know roughly how long a manufacturing plant will last, there is also a marketplace for equipment that will wear out faster than the old stuff.

I've linked a paper in the links and references on the topic of imported electrical transformers being plugged into our grid, from the Department of Homeland Security to give you something to think about. Imports of these items are considered an "extraordinary and unusual threat" to national security.

The same goes for any piece of equipment with a computer chip in it. Counterfeit and knockoff computer chips are rampant.

That being the case, this problem will never go away, but may very well get worse.

Vintage Tools vs. Today's Tools

https://www.youtube.com/watch?v=iBgGJwvc8lQ

The Reliability Culture

This is a strategy to consciously dedicate resources to the most practical long-term maintenance strategy that is appropriate for the business. The skills for this are different from turning a wrench, and part of the reason that this has met with some resistance is that maintenance managers tend to be former wrench-turners rather than data analysts.

The way this works is that there is a portal or software of some kind that has on it a database for all of the company's equipment. It keeps track of the amount of maintenance that has to be done, so that the company knows how often to lubricate and change out consumable items like filters.

What eventually happens is that they learn how costly a given piece of equipment is to maintain, and make decisions based on data as to when, if ever it is time to get rid of it and get a better one.

The "pro" of this system is that it helps you make better decisions, but the "con" is that it relies on maintenance employees to do their jobs properly, regarding data entry, logging in to the system and filling out entries, and other jobs that this type of person typically hates.

So, the data comes at a cost. In most companies of less than about 100 employees, particularly if the project is labor-intense such as hand assembly, it works marginally.

This method is much better in refineries and chemical plants which are continuous process operations. At those places, they are fanatic about tracking machine downtime, and they can track maintenance versus lost production time, and prioritize on that basis. It is common for a refinery with 100 employees to have as many as 10 maintenance people, whose job it is to monitor equipment and make things nice and robust.

The Family Business and Farm Model
In these businesses, the model is different. The supervisor, if there is one, walks around with a pair of pliers and screwdriver in his or her pocket, and makes adjustments on the fly. This goes particularly for a farmer, because there

is no such thing as calling a mechanic when your belt has slipped off in the middle of a corn field somewhere.

But a human is still doing the job, and even farmers occasionally screw up.

Farm Girl Video

https://www.youtube.com/watch?v=qzlcU5EHLW4

If the problem is serious, the normal mode for a small business is to outsource some maintenance activity, with all of the advantages and disadvantages we will talk about regarding this form of "organization."

Equipment Failure

Maintenance, like other activities, is done by humans. Humans have to engineer, purchase, install and maintain production equipment. This equipment is "fixed" but the marketplace is subject to change especially by increasing the need to improve throughput and reduce cost, and at the same time, in many industries, improve precision.

There is an ongoing issue with people doing their jobs, as we said, and ultimately, when a piece of equipment breaks down, some human is at the root of it all.

What is going to happen in the future? Well, I predict that this problem will get much worse. We're currently in the process of onshoring or importing to Mexico all of the manufacturing we used to manufacture in China. My favorite talking head on this is Peter Zeihan:

Peter Zeihan ref: reshoring manufacturing

https://www.youtube.com/watch?v=UNxkpqx1LDw

That's part of why I am writing this.

As we scale back up, you can expect the ability to turn a wrench to become more valuable than it was, and stuff to break down, and the world to be less reliable. Think about the power grid.

Further Thought Question

What happens when the above Dividend Growth Model falls apart? What happens when the population no longer grows? What happens when the value of a business is not related to its growth?

Well, I predict that what happens is the same thing that happens to farmers. When something breaks you fix it until you can't. This is beyond my scope at the moment, but it is something that is out there, as the post-growth people will tell you.

Links and References

12 Low Wage Workers

We're going to need to give some consideration to Low Wage Workers. Life is difficult for these people, and they don't all have the same attitude toward their condition.

Some fraction of the low wage workforce sails along singing and happy, because that is who they are. Some are in a constant state of desperation. Some others are very angry, because at some point, they've lost "hope."

But it's hard to get low wage workers to do their jobs. A lot of the little problems we bump into during the course of the day happen because of the failure of some low wage worker to do his or her job.

Definition of Low Wage Workers

The Harvard Business Review defines "Low Wage Worker" as anyone that makes less than about $40,000 a year. Of course, this varies slightly depending on what part of the country we're talking about.

This is twice the level of the US Poverty Line. The current US Poverty Line is about $14,000 per year, which would make this about $7 an hour, for those that are working 52 weeks per year.

The current US Minimum Wage is $7.25 an hour, so you'd have to work full time, and you'd still be "poor." One thing employers do is limit the number of hours that an employee can work, so that they don't have to pay benefits. So, it is common enough for people to work two or more low wage jobs.

The current US "Livable Wage" varies depending on what part of the country you're living in, but according to Zip Recruiter, it's around $26 per hour on average. That's the amount of money it takes to live in a place, have transportation, and have food and medical care today.

The "Average American Income" at the current time is $71,000 per year, but the "Average American" believes that it should be about $85,000 to "get by" according to a poll quoted in "The Hill."

There's a Bureau of Labor Statistics publication linked in the links and references that tells you who these "average people" are.

https://youtu.be/gTJhlVFyvm8

Polluted Labor Pool

Why People Don't Do Their Jobs

Intelligence

There was a book written in the 1990s that was, as we now say "canceled" to the effect that there is a strong correlation between income and intelligence.

This should come as no surprise to anyone who has tried to get a low wage worker to do a complex job.

The current talking heads have a lot to say about this, and we have cited them elsewhere, to the effect that since 15% of the population, by definition, has an IQ of under 85, we're going to have a hell of a problem when jobs become so complex that it takes high reasoning skills to do them.

What that means is that a significant portion of the population is in, and stuck in, low wage jobs permanently. According to the study I linked a person that is in a low wage job for 10 years or more has less than a 2% chance of getting out. That whole situation is very likely to get worse post-pandemic.

Issues with Low Wage Employees

Here are some possible issues for low wage employees, from various sources. These might be the cause of some of these people not showing up for work and/or not doing their jobs.

Issue	Comments
Transportation	Significant issue for low wage employees, public transit availability is a plus to retain these workers.
Caregiver Issues	Because 59% of low wage workers are women, this is a significant issue for kids or elderly relatives.
Health Care	Due to health care disparities, low wage workers and their families are more susceptible to illness. Obesity is significantly higher for lower income women.
Mental Health	Prevalence of depression in low wage workers is as high as 19% vs. 17% in the general population.
Immigrants	20% of low wage workers are immigrants, with resulting language and cultural issues.

Government Response

This is a bit of a political hot potato, and I do have a few things to say about it.

In Georgia, about 4,000 of the 66,000 total employees in the state for Wal Mart Corporation take part in the SNAP program, and Medicaid benefits. People have pointed out that this amounts to a subsidy from the government that enables a low wage labor force to work at this place plus McDonalds, two of the largest employers of low wage workers.

In the case of Atlanta, and most similar cities, public transportation is also heavily subsidized. The current deficit for this system is on the order of $1 billion, which if you divide by the 57 million rides, comes out to about $17 per ride, which is an hour's work for a low wage worker.

There's a third subsidy, Section 8 housing, which comes to an additional $412 million in Atlanta, which is just the tip of the iceberg nationwide.

You may feel free to argue all you want about the magnitude of this, but it is significant, and it is a benefit to the companies like Wally Mart and McDonalds, and the baggage handlers at the Atlanta airport and a lot of the low wage workers that work at your local pizza place. Since we're financing a lot of this right now by deficit spending, it amounts to a transfer of wealth from the future taxpayers to the major corporations.

FYI the average wage of a Wal Mart worker in Georgia is $18.53 per hour. The average wage of the Kia Plant in Georgia is (drum roll) $18.

What are we to make of all of this?
I am ready to say that there is a vast population of low wage workers. It is hard to get low wage workers to do their jobs.

This problem is only going to get worse going forward. Any robotics, automated robot drivers, and robot anything else is going to target this already vulnerable labor force. There is an overall decline in real income in the US since 1974, for the bottom 60% of the labor force, as we have said earlier.

This has gone on throughout history. Dickens and Upton Sinclair, along with Nicolò Machiavelli have all written about it at length. It is a very famous topic of literature. There will always be working poor. If you've been around a little, like I have, you'll see the nations' attitude toward them. We have already talked about McCaig's Law, and the same applies to a nation. You can tell everything you need to know about a nation by how it treats its low wage workers.

A lot of the social systems that are now in place were put there as a subsidy for business and to keep the cities from burning down like they did in 1968, and very nearly did in 1937, and yet again in 2020 and 2021.

When the situation gets out of hand, like it will, it is going to cause a lot of problems. In my opinion, only one thing is missing, namely a leader. Whether the leader turns out to be Evita or Gandhi, or Ferdinand Marcos is an open question.

Links and References

13 Top Gun Pilots

Top Gun Pilots are super-people. They are at the human peak of dexterity, reaction time, courage, and intelligence. But as I am about to explain to you, it is hard to get them to do their jobs.

I have seen some interviews with "real" Top Gun Pilots, by the way. Nowadays they seem aware of their intellectual and physical gifts, and are a bit humble, from what I saw. This is more directed toward the "movie" version of Top Gun Pilots who disobey orders, are internally competitive, wreck planes, and flirt with young females.

Here's a rule: No one ever made a movie about people that were cooperative, did what they were told all the time, and never got into danger.

What is Top Gun?

Top Gun is the US Navy "Strike Fighter Tactics Instructor Program." The idea is that the Navy brass would assemble the most proficient navy pilots, train them in some best practices as to how to do dogfighting and other stunts, and then send them back to their units.

To get in, you must make it as a Navy fighter pilot and be considered proficient enough within your unit to be recommended by your commander.

https://youtu.be/lE_TNBVXwvg

So maybe the top 5% of the already select population are chosen, and those people also need to have some teaching ability, to take the methods back to their unit.

Among these, a further small fraction is later invited back to be instructors.

High Performers
Top Gun Pilots are the fraction of the workforce in many fields that are high performers. Laurence J. Peter calls them the "super competent." The world sends these people a different message from an early age. We all know people like that.

They think they're smarter than everybody because they are. They don't read directions, take educated risks, and outsmart the system because they can.

But it's hard to get them to do their jobs.

In fact, in the Peter Principle, Peter states that in the hierarchy, these are the only people that are likely to be fired. If you are merely incompetent or mediocre at your job, you aren't a threat to anybody. But if you are super competent, you're a threat to the hierarchy, and therefore violate the prime rule, which is "The Hierarchy Must Be Preserved."

Personality Indicators

The Myers Briggs Type Indicator is the most popular method of assessing personality. This method rates people in four different personality aspects based on the answers to a survey. The variables are introvert/extrovert I/E, Intuition/Sensing (N/S) Thinking/Feeling (T/F) and Perceptive/Judgmental (P/J).

Some psychologists are negative on this method because it doesn't predict any sort of success in the workplace, per this video:

Personality Tests

https://youtu.be/-Z8J9edf_gw?si=vKzLaeC6To2mo2dw

The "pilot" Myers-Briggs type is ISTJ, which is introverted, sensing, thinking and judgmental, for those who wish to follow along.

Enneagram: The Enneagram Institute has developed this system of personality description, based on 9 fundamental characteristics, also based on a survey. These types are listed in the diagram below. People have a primary characteristic and a "wing" which is a further descriptor.

The Enneagram with Riso-Hudson Type Names

There is no real suggestion that this method is useful for anything besides entertainment, but for what it is worth, the pilot is considered a 7, which is spontaneous, inquisitive, versatile and scattered.

Big Five Indicators: Some experts believe that there is data supporting this method, which characterizes people based on five basic characteristics: This method was coined in 1949 by D. W. Fiske. The characteristics are extroversion, agreeableness, openness, conscientiousness, and neuroticism. A subject is rated on each one of these, and there is data to the effect that they are predictors in the workplace. It is more correct to say, as we will find out later, that the workplace and the personality need to fit.

The Top Gun Pilots of the world rate high on openness, conscientiousness and extroversion, and neuroticism is practically unheard of in this group, which I guess makes sense.

Aircraft Accidents

Here is where I am going with all of this. According to Wisner Baum, the trial lawyers, 88% of chartered aircraft crashes are caused by pilot error. That means that the most highly trained people in the system are the ones that are causing the problems.

According to the Flight Safety Council up to 40% of failures in approach and landing were caused by pilots deliberately not following the Standard Operating Procedure. There is general agreement that pilots deliberately not following the SOP is a significant cause of failure.

I've linked several references to try to figure out what percentage of the time the pilots deliberately violate the rules, and not crash. That would be the more interesting piece of data because that would tell how prevalent the practice is. But naturally the data is a little hard to come by. No one wants to admit it, and no one wants to publicly announce that their pilots break the rules all the time.

Also, it is true that the air pilots need to follow a lot of non-flight-related rules, including work hour limitations, alcohol and drug consumption, and simple instructions from air traffic controllers.

But let's just say hypothetically it happens a significant percentage of the time.

Reasons for Pilots Not Following the SOP

This has been heavily studied, and in the links, there are several good articles to this effect. One of the better ones cites the following reasons that a pilot might not want to do this:

Anti-authority

Impulsiveness

Invulnerability

Machismo

Resignation

Complacency

If you would care to go back to the chapter on speeding, you will see a lot of parallels.

Another one commonly mentioned is the idea that the pilot is better aware of the best way of operating the plane, and why it is perfectly fine to buzz the tower a few times at the end of a long day of flying.

The pioneering book "Human Factors in Multi Crew Flight Operations" by Orlady lists four main factors, which are pretty much the same thing:

Improvement

Malevolent

Hedonic

Indolent

Which is to say that the bad kids will think they are cool. They haven't evolved much since the seventh grade.

Prevention Methods

There have been constant efforts to "train" and "correct" these Top Gun Pilots, but it doesn't usually work.

The most effective method is something called "PINC" training, which stands for Procedural Intentional Non-Compliance. In this type of training, the pilot is sat down in a chair with a light shining on him and told the following:

We know what you're doing and why.

Here are the risks you are taking

Your peer group will negatively be affected by it.

David Huntzinger, air safety expert, is a consultant that specializes in this sort of thing as it applies to air crews and believes about ⅔ of it can be done away with.

Current Developments

In fact, we have entered an era where commercial airline accidents have reached the lowest level in many years. At the same time, the number of airline pilots with no military experience has gone from ⅓ to nearly ⅔.

I am not prepared to make this argument for causality, and I will invite any PhD candidate who wants to make the causal argument to contribute to this body of knowledge. In support of this I have linked a Reddit thread in the links and references, to the effect that even though there were a lot of workplace SOP in the military air training system, there was minimal if any enforcement. I am ready to say that someone who wants to be a pilot nowadays, who needs to get required flight hours and pay for them is unlikely to buzz the tower.

I will also say that at the current moment, because of the retirement of a lot of the Vietnam and Desert Storm pilots, there are a lot fewer people around who have been shot at while flying, at least in North America. PTSD is real.

The case of Randall "Duke" Cunningham
While we are on the topic of Vietnam fighter pilots, I would point out the interesting case of Randall "Duke" Cunningham.

This fellow was the first fighter ace for the US Navy in Vietnam and was featured on the NOVA series "Top Gun and Beyond." I have a couple of videos linked below.

Cunningham later became an instructor at the "Top Gun" flight school. Yes, he actually was a "Top Gun Pilot."

He later ran for US Congress and won. At some point, he began actively soliciting and accepting bribes from defense contractors. This was eventually uncovered by reporters, Cunningham pleaded guilty, and served eight years in the joint, and on his release, asked to receive special permission to buy a firearm, so that he could hunker down in a place in Arkansas.

There is a book about this fellow, The Wrong Stuff, which I have linked below.

Duke Cunningham Bio

https://www.amazon.com/Wrong-Stuff-Extraordinary-Cunningham-Congressman/dp/B001G7RCX4

Duke Cunningham Video

https://youtu.be/OqApSPbNifU?si=l_yZt-MzaDR0-who

Duke Cunningham Out on Parole

https://youtu.be/4qCHGVhgWf8?si=WOnzsK75PSyoErLa

Draw whatever conclusions you will from this interesting character.

If you care to do a search on the topic "top gun pilot sentenced to prison" you will see that despite being a very small fraction of the population, there are multiple instances of this group being locked up for one reason or another.

Tailhook

There is another article from Military dot com that says that thanks to the original Top Gun movie, there was a significant uptick in recruiting for Navy pilots.

Also, a culture of reckless misbehavior was blamed for the "Tailhook Scandal" which was a series of incidents that occurred at a convention of these people. In this convention of Top Gun Pilots, 83 women and 7 men were alleged to have been sexually assaulted in a hotel in Vegas.

Quality Systems conventions are much more boring. The last one I went to was in a hotel in Cleveland, and no one got arrested.

Top Gun Pilots

First, however hard it is to get "regular people" to do their jobs, it is particularly difficult in the case of the Top Gun Pilot.

Some of these people are very humble and understand where they are in the world. But there are a lot of brats who will break the rules because they can.

Here's another rule: People do what they do, until they can't, and then they do something else.

Why People Don't Do Their Jobs

Links and References

14 Why the Airline Killed Your Dog and Lost Your Bag

We're going to talk about why the Airline killed your dog and lost your bag. These two issues are an artifact of how the airlines work, as we will find out, and there are some common threads.

To be perfectly honest, a lot of us have stories about airlines not doing their jobs right now. The airlines have a complex job, which is to successfully move people from place to place on a huge scale.

We have talked about McCaig's Law, which, broadly applied, says that nothing happens in isolation. It is rare for an organization to be incompetent at something like baggage handling and be good at everything else. It's more likely for them to be incompetent at everything.

I've attached a video link that explains this.

Flying Experience

To start with, if I total all my airline miles, I am around 2 million, including a lot of international travel. I also have a couple of companies as clients in my consulting business that do some recruiting and outsourcing for one of the airlines downtown.

I pick on the airlines all the time, for good reason.

Air Travel in General

Air travel is popular. It has a lot of knock-on effects in the cities with big airports. It makes people happy. It is an indirect subsidy to businesses such as the NFL and the gaming industry. There are rental cars and Starbucks around the airports. So, the USA and a lot of other nations subsidize this activity through government involvement.

In Europe and Asia, the governments don't hide this at all. Air travel is considered an essential service, so they are part owners of the national airlines.

But it would be a worthwhile PhD project for someone to come up with the per-ticket subsidy for air travel in the US. To do this you would have to include direct payments, indirect payments, and other benefits that the airlines get from the "taxpayers."

Socialism?

Funneling money directly into an industry is considered "socialism" and we don't do that. Instead, we do airline bailouts every time the airlines get into trouble, and also, there is ongoing government help for "infrastructure."

There is such a thing as the "Essential Air Subsidy" program, which started in 1979 when the industry was "deregulated." The government pays up to $100 a ticket per passenger to get them to fly into little airports like Trenton. The fare on Frontier from Atlanta to Trenton on a good day is $17 and it would be insane from a business point of view for the company to have this. But because of the subsidy, they're able to keep the Trenton airport open, even though it is only about 40 miles from the Philadelphia airport.

The whole system is full of little back door subsidies. American Airlines reported $147 million in profits last year despite getting $293 million in subsidies.

The point is, we've long ago left the point at which "market forces" are allowed to drive the system. It's considered politically acceptable because of the indirect benefits, and "they" are careful not to call it what it is.

Who Benefits?

Well, to start with, the defense industry. Do you think that Boeing and Lockheed would make as much money as they do without the airlines replacing their fleet every few years? It's an indirect subsidy to them, so that they continue to build stealth bombers.

But in addition to that, a lot of other businesses benefit. Back in the early 90's the company I worked for had a sales office in the place where their biggest customer's HQ is. There are examples of this today in Bentonville Arkansas, where the HQ for Wal Mart is.

Someone got the bright idea that the same thing could be accomplished by closing the remote offices and running everything out of Atlanta. They cleared several million dollars out of their overhead because they found out that if you wanted a customer meeting you could just fly up for the day.

A lot of companies did that. Now that there's teleworking, there is a paradigm shift in this, too, but we will have to see how that turns out.

Airline Indifference to Customers

I guess it goes without saying that the airline business is both owned and operated by top gun pilots, literally. That's how the image of the airline pilot in the tidy uniform happened as a symbol of power.

To the extent that I can tell, the pilots themselves are overworked and at this point it is not glamorous. Neither is the job of flight attendant. But there is an immense amount of overhead activity like ticket clerks and customer service people in this period that is directly customer facing. This is the part that is really annoying for consumers. This, coupled with the fact that the government persists in bailing out the system, is a fact of the industry.

When we want to know the public attitude about something, we'll just use our favorite search engine to see how many search results we get for various phrases:

Search	Results
The airline treated me fairly	2,430,000
The airline gave me good service	3,080,000
I called the airline and talked to a person	1,270,000
The airline solved my problem	5,790,000
The airline cares about me	10,500,000
The airline made me happy	25,700,000

Search	Results

The airline treated me unfairly	2,100,000
The airline gave me poor service	830,000
I called the airline and never talked to a person	1,860,000
The airline did not solve my problem	11,300,000
The airline does not care about me	31,900,000
The airline made me mad	19,900,000

So here it is. About twice as many people said that the airline didn't solve their problem, and about three times as many people said that the airline doesn't care about them.

In light of that, let's continue with our story.

Why the Airlines Killed Your Dog

Pet travel has its origins back in the dark ages, namely 1989. Prior to that it wasn't really a "thing" to travel with your pet.

The practice grew in popularity though, as the number of casual fliers increased. The airlines were fine with this at first. It encouraged people to travel.

It looks like the turning point was in the 2014–2015-time frame.

At about that time, it was determined by someone that "Emotional Support Animals" were equivalent to "Service Animals. Who made the decision is not completely clear, but we now can attribute this to the "Amorphous They" that work somewhere in the airlines.

We will spend some time on the "Amorphous They" a little later.

The reason this matters is that you could produce a note from your shrink that says that you "need" to travel with your emotional support animal. If you could do that, the airlines would let you take your dog, cat, potbellied pig, pea fowl, snake, or whatever animal calmed you down without charging you.

What then happened was that this sort of thing exploded in popularity. In retrospect, we should have seen it for what it was. A doctor's visit was cheaper than putting your dog into a kennel.

Prior to 2014 there were no real statistics available on the incidence of this, but in 2015 there were around 534,000 pet flights, which is when this sort of thing reached its peak.

You can see what happened. Nobody in the system knew what they were doing. There was no standard operating procedure for "emotional support animals." Flight attendants, baggage handlers and the public were not thinking clearly.

Year	"Incidents"	Incidents per

		10,000 trips
2022	9	0.48
2021	21	0.82
2020	10	0.32
2019	19	0.47
2018	17	0.40
2017	40	0.79
2016	48	0.92
2015	63	1.18

Why the Airline Killed Your Dog

Now we have the whole story. The airline killed your dog because of the following:

"They" didn't clearly think through the policy

There was no thought put into the standard operating procedure

There was minimal training of personnel to deal with 534,000 animals during flights

Clearer Thinking

If "they" had been thinking clearly, they'd have said "What are we doing?"

Nothing alive should travel in the cargo hold of an aircraft, even though it is pressurized. In fact, an argument can be made that nothing alive should travel in the main cabin.

Furthermore, nothing that can pee should travel in an overhead bin.

And those ugly little dogs that were bred to have no noses had no business being exposed to a low-oxygen environment, on the ground or anywhere.

What then happened was an interesting event. People started saying "no."

The big decline in air travel during Covid was an opportunity to change the system. The airlines each enacted more highly restrictive animal travel policies. I have another link in the links and references that you can follow to get the current airline animal policy.

To make a long story short, "emotional support" animals are now just considered "animals". You're no longer allowed to bring your pig on a flight. Animals are restricted to cats and dogs. If you want to bring your dog along, you need to fill out four forms, take it to the vet and make sure it's healthy, and have it be no bigger than fitting under your seat.

Plus, the airlines will now charge you $125 each way to bring your pet, which is roughly what a kennel will cost you.

So, once that all happened, it got to be much less of a problem. The number of trips by animals decreased by about 60%, down to 188,000 in 2022, and about 90% of the problem went away.

https://youtu.be/HvAxmhNpA1A

Why the Airline Lost Your Bag

We're ready to deal with this problem, which is interesting in that a slightly different set of people is involved, but there is some overlap. This problem is current, as of 2024.

In a general way, here is why people aren't doing their jobs, and are losing bags.

Measurements are incomplete and questionable

People, especially baggage handlers are disengaged.

Airport infrastructure is overloaded, (especially IT infrastructure)

General industry mayhem (Nothing Happens in Isolation)

First, how big of a problem is this?

The US Department of Transportation has a web page on this topic, and provides you with a spreadsheet, which I have linked in the links and references. That data is incomplete and iffy, for two reasons. One is that they rely on the airlines to report this stuff "voluntarily" and another is that the most recent data is from 2022.

There is one interesting piece of data though. You can compare 2019, the last "normal" pre-Covid year, and 2022. Here is a table.

Statistic	2019	2022
Passengers Enplaned (Millions)	860	791
Baggage Enplaned	506 million	470 million
Bag loss Rate (reports per 1000 passengers)	3.45%	3.78%

There is an article from The Guardian in the links that says that the percentage of lost bags doubled globally between 2019 and 2022 but that data is also tainted since it came from SITA, which is a company that sells baggage insurance. What we do know about SITA is that they do a good job of publicizing their service.

So already there is an issue of reliable data to be able to measure the problem. As Deming would say, you can't change what you don't measure. What we do know is that apparently, we are stupid. Despite the increased perceived rate of bag loss, people are still checking their bags.

There is a lot of anecdotal evidence which I have cited below, regarding baggage failure, particularly on international flights.

If you search "the airline lost my bag" you get about 6.1 million hits.

Employees are Disengaged

This is the one everybody talks about, and there is some element of truth to it. Who are the baggage handlers? These are 18–40-year-old males, who didn't pay attention in math class. They have the hard job of taking your awkwardly packed and overstuffed bag and throwing it into the hold of an airplane.

Do you want that job? I certainly don't. I for sure don't want to do it at midnight on some snowy runway in Cleveland.

Here's a job description and an actual job review on Indeed.

Full Time Airport Baggage Handler

⋮

Unifi Aviation, LLC

Atlanta, GA 30354 (Lakewood Heights-Southeastern area)

$15 an hour   **Full-time**

Responsibilities Ensures proper conveyances set up to sort and distribute incoming bags. Reads and verifies the city and flight number for every bag to ensure...

Active 10 days ago

1.0   **Unifi**

★☆☆☆☆   Ramp Agent (Former Employee) - Dulles - July 18, 2023

I worked for Unifi in both ECP and IAD locations. ECP is fine, but IAD is probably one of the worst ran locations I've ever seen. The management don't have a clue on what's going on, you're on your own on the first day at work, want you to pay for your own parking in the training period (which can add up fast), or they tell you in park at a near by hotel & risk getting your car towed by the hotel (shady). They wonder why the turn over rate is so high. If you in need of a job, that's understandable. You will just spend more in parking than what the job is worth. I was having problems with logging in on training on my first day & no one in management tried to help or set anything up. Took me three & a half hours troubleshooting & finding phone numbers to tech support to get started on my training. Workers without badges will have to be put up by management & they would be waiting for one to one & a half hours to be picked up.

✓ **Pros**

None, maybe flight benefits.

✗ **Cons**

Too many to count.

A Day in the Life of a Baggage Handler

This job pays $15 an hour, they don't pay for your car or parking, and you're undermanaged and doing heavy lifting. Are you showing up for work? Me neither. An apartment in Atlanta rents for $1800 a month, so you have to sleep in your mom's basement, because a 40-hour work week will only get you $2400 a month, and if you also have to pay for a car that's not enough to break even.

My favorite talking head on this is Nicholas Eberstadt.

Nicholas Eberstadt Interview

https://youtu.be/Zp1qoUxwMzQ?si=Rjh1merQCOssrOW1

It is people like the baggage handlers who provide me with a revenue stream. They're poorly trained, underpaid, disengaged in the workforce and cause a lot of quality issues. They also get into mischief, substance abuse and at some point, get ticked off and/or hurt. The particular ad is for something called Unifi, which is an outsourcing agency. Is this the employees' fault? There are serious systemic problems in rewarding people who work hard to make sure you get your bags.

This is an enormous untapped resource. which is a loss to the people who like their baggage to arrive on time.

If it makes you feel any better, which it shouldn't, the problem extends up the food chain.

It goes higher than the Baggage Handler

There's a story linked in the links and references about a lady that, after repeated calls to the airline, flew to Chicago because the airline couldn't track her valuable lacrosse sticks. She had attached one of those "air tags" to it and couldn't find a competent customer service person who would help her.

There's another story of a passenger who used an air tag to track his or her bag to a dumpster behind a sketchy apartment. Hers, and a lot of other bags had been stolen, apparently by the bag handlers themselves. Passengers are now better able to keep track of this than the airlines and solve their own "Case of the Missing Luggage."

Infrastructure issues

If you go farther back, to about 2011 to 2019 and compare the data, you can see that the number of people doing air travel has increased greatly.

Statistic	2011	2019
Passengers Enplaned	514	860
Bags Explained	?	508
Lost Bags	1.72	?
Lost Bags (reports per 1000 passengers)	3.35	?

This data is fairly confusing because of the gaps except for one thing. The amount of air travel increased by 67% during that time.

Since 2011, has there been any new airport construction? According to the references below, there was exactly one new commercial airport opened since then, and that's up by Minot in the North Dakota oil fields. Your airport is out of capacity.

There are a couple of stories below, per the recent infrastructure bill that was enacted by the US Government. If you read through these, most of the "infrastructure" expenditures are for bigger parking lots and cushier terminals. There is little or no talk about baggage handling equipment, because I guess it is invisible.

I am ready to throw out the idea that despite the big increase in air travel, there is no big increase in baggage equipment.

IT infrastructure is an integral part of this as well. The airlines are just like the rest of us, who hate to upgrade their IT equipment. The whole aircraft ticketing system was developed sometime in the 1980's. There was a meltdown lately of the FAA IT system which caused general industry grounding. This is attributable to a corrupted database on an old system.

Repeated attempts to modernize it have been marginally successful, as the article I've linked says. The people who set up the system in the first place are on the brink of retirement.

Here's a quote:

"These systems were built at a time when the airlines may have been smaller, and they weren't necessarily built to handle so much data coming in at once," the official said. "When you have something like the massive winter storm over the holidays, it cannot handle the volume of changes coming in at one time, because it's on a system that wasn't built to handle that large of a moving dataset."

Problem Four: General Industry Mayhem

The best example of this is the problem with Southwest Airlines, that happened just before Christmas 2022.

Southwest had been slow to upgrade their IT systems. This was due to a few bad years due to Covid but also because they have fewer resources than their entrenched competitors.

For a period of a week or so, the whole company basically had to shut down because the system that schedules their crews "melted down." According to the article I have linked in the links, there were 15,000 flights canceled, and it was considered the largest airline meltdown of its type in history.

The attributed reasons were the IT issues, and, their underlying business strategy which avoids the "hub and spoke" system.

There's a reference in the links and references from Insure MyFlight.com, which is a company that will sell you flight insurance. These are the people that make it their business to know how often flights are canceled. In that article, it says that around 4% of the flights are canceled from the worst airports. According to that article around ⅓ of all flights are delayed in places like Honolulu and Las Vegas, and in the best performing, something on the order of 16%.

Here's a graphic:

U.S. Airports with Highest Percentage of Flight Delays in 2023

1. HNL - 29.8% Daniel K. Inouye International Airport Honolulu

2. LAS - 28.6% Las Vegas Airport Harry Reid International Airport

3. SFO - 28.4% San Francisco International

4. PBI - 27.7% Palm Beach International

5. OGG - 27.5% Official Kahului Airport

6. LIH - 26.5% Lihue Airport Kauai

7. SJU - 26.3% San Juan Airport - Luis Muñoz Marín International

8. FLL - 26.0% Fort Lauderdale–Hollywood International

9. MCO - 26.0% Orlando International Airport

10. SAN - 25.6% San Diego International Airport

Because of general mayhem in this industry, including a significant number of flights canceled and delayed, no wonder bags get lost and are late. Missing luggage happens because you and the plane are late yourselves.

Murdered Animals and Lost Luggage

In most businesses, if there was a failure rate somewhere between 3% and 19% the company would go broke. The failure rate on the bag claim activity is about at those levels, and it is only because of enormous subsidies that it is that low.

From the government's point of view, they want the airlines and airports to exist magically, the airlines themselves are hard pressed to improve, and the whole system has reached its useful lifespan.

Lost Luggage and Other First World Problems

I think that this is another one of these cases of fundamental problems with the business model. We are choosing to prop up this luxurious form of travel because we like it. It does come at a cost, ultimately, which is partly paid for by taxpayers and/or being balanced on the shoulders of the proletariat, as Marx would say.

Also, this is another system that is so big and so established we can no longer do without it without a lot of whining and drama.

But here is another case where the traditional solution of "trusting the free market" no longer works. Air travel has evolved into something approaching a necessity for some people.

So here is the bottom line. The Airlines kill your dog and lose your bag because we, as a society allow it. In the grand scheme of things, no one is saying "I'm going to drive to Cleveland next time because there is a 30% chance my flight will be late and a 5% chance my bag will get lost." They will accept the risk for the time being because the alternative, driving, is less pleasant.

That being the case, the people that own the system, which is the airlines and the airports, aren't going to change because there is no economic incentive for them to do so. Do you want proof? The number of crashes on aircraft is at an all-time low. Why? Because the airlines "try." There is an enormous publicity issue with having their planes fall out of the sky, so they go to great lengths to not have it.

Other than getting you there, this is the same mentality as the phone company and the bank. You need them, and they don't need you.

Sorry about the late bag. There is a way to fix it but it requires change. There is a cry from some of these people to re-regulate, but the government usually doesn't fix anything.

You know what might work? What if you pay another $100 per ticket for some assurance that your dog and bag will make it and your plane will be on time. The airline might distribute this money to the baggage crew and the flight attendants to motivate them.

Links and References

15 Why Your Hometown Exploded

In February of 2023, there was a huge train wreck and massive explosion that polluted the little town of East Palestine, Ohio.

At the time I am writing this, the investigation is still underway, but the effects on the town will be very long lasting.

We also know exactly what questions the lawyers are going to ask, because the lawsuits have just begun to fly.

My Railroad Connection
I am a former railroad employee, both my dad and grandfather had over 40 years of experience in railroading. Plus, I have a lot of work experience in and around bulk loading and unloading platforms in the chemical business.

I've audited a dozen or so refineries and/or producers of lethal chemicals as an ISO auditor.

So, I know the thought process.

I've also spent a week in the locomotive factory and audited some railroad-related distribution facilities. Plus, I know a lot about human failure.

The East Palestine Train Disaster

A train was traveling between Madison, Illinois and Conway PA. This train was traveling on a main line, and was 1.76 miles long, according to Wikipedia. It had somewhere around 150 cars. Twenty of these were carrying various hazardous materials. This included some benzene, which is on the nasty end of the scale regarding chemicals.

When it reached the town of Salem, Ohio, it passed over a "defect detector" which indicated that one of the cars had caught on fire. A security video along the tracks indicated a condition the railroaders call a "hot box", that is, overheated wheel bearing. The suspect car was carrying a load of plastic pallets.

Rail Disaster Security Cam

https://youtu.be/J5rhdOTcVso

It took about 20 minutes for the train operators, who were in a locomotive at the front of the train, to get the alarm, and put on the brakes. The wreck happened in East Palestine, OH.

When they "put on the brakes" they didn't fool around, according to the sources in the links and references. They applied braking, and emergency braking to slow the whole thing down. It's hard to slow a 2-mile-long train down. There is no talk of how fast it was going at the time but unless otherwise found out, it is usually between 40 and 50 MPH.

What that caused was a massive jackknifing situation. Railroad personnel and emergency crews arrived, and over 70 first responders from the area worked the blaze. The huge fire burned for two days. There were initial assurances that all was well, and people should stay in their homes, and conflicting evacuation orders a few days later.

Lasting Effects
The town itself was permanently affected.

The local EPA and state officials had to dispose of millions of gallons of contaminated dirt and water that was generated during the fire. Locals are concerned that there are still toxic fumes in the area, which there obviously are.

The railroad managed to get things back running on February 9th, but obviously the residents weren't happy about it.

Effects on People
The residents of East Palestine OH are still being affected as well. A lot of them have complained about health effects. This was sort of a vulnerable population anyway, like small town Ohio people are.

The lawsuits are just now starting to fly. Erin Brockovich reported on the scene. The local politicians, who were previously all for deregulation and pro-business, have suddenly turned environmentalists.

The effects of this will last for years. Every case of cancer in town will be blamed on this disaster.

Let's Start with the Locomotive Engineer
The engineer of these things is just like an airline pilot, right? They must have years of experience, are highly trained, have a federal license, and extensive simulator testing, right?

Well, it looks like there is some standardization, and they won't just hire these people off the street. The typical career path is to start as a $25 per hour conductor, which they do hire off the street.

As part of the initial training there is a Federal Railroad Administration test that the employees need to complete that tells them the basics. According to the FAQ's I posted in the links and references, the job of "Locomotive Engineer" is determined by seniority. Norfolk Southern is about 3/4 unionized.

He, probably he, probably got his job by seniority, rather than some special ability to operate a dangerous, 2-mile-long motor vehicle with 20 cars of hazardous material in it

According to the FAQ that I have attached in the references, once the "conductor" has enough seniority, they can bid on the "Extra Board" which means that they can get a short gig as a locomotive engineer for a shift or two, which could include nights and holidays. Once they build up time, as they say, they can bid on more steady work.

The identity and work experience of the actual guys who were running this train at the time have not been released yet.

There were three people in the train at the time, the locomotive engineer, a conductor, and a "trainee." There is a shortage of this type of worker. The hours are terrible, you have to work in the cold and dark. You're expected to be able to read and write, but there are no special qualifications.

Engineer Simulator

https://youtu.be/QlxYu8G9NMI

The Evening Shift

So here is the situation. The accident occurred at about 9 PM. It's 600 miles between Madison IL to Salem, Ohio, which is more than the 12-hour limit for a train crew. So, this crew must have started their shift along the way.

From their point of view, it's cold, 9 PM, and dark. You got on at someplace like Indianapolis, and you've been on this thing for 10 hours. It's 39 miles between Salem Ohio and the final destination, Conway PA. So, let's go out on a limb and say that they were at the end of their shift and possibly exhausted.

Does the training and train simulator cover a situation where it is cold, 9 PM, and you have been on the train for 10 or more hours? Unlikely.

The long-term trend in this industry is to try to reduce costs. Therefore, whereas a train had a crew of 5 people in 1960, they only have 2 now. Part of this is the reliance on electronics and other equipment that provide additional safety.

Impaired Workers

Sleep deprivation is a form of workplace impairment that is at least as serious as any others.

Locomotive Engineer Investigation: To Do List

So, if we were investigating this, for some legal reason, we could get together a to-do list, like this:

Topic	Question	Investigation
Training	Was the operator trained?	Look for training records, how long ago since training? What are the requirements for recertification?
Physical Condition	Was the operator impaired?	How long had the operator been on the train? How long since his previous shift? How many hours had he worked in the last day? What about the last month? Was he, or was he not, "impaired" or did he have "diminished function."
Experience	How much experience?	How many similar situations? The records of previous trips can and will be examined to see if this fellow is "accident prone."
Human Factor Management	Was the operator ticked off?	What was the psychological condition of the operator at the time of the decision to flip on the brakes? We would look for records of disciplinary action, performance reviews, and interviews with bosses and fellow workers.
Procedural	Did the	The controls of these

Awareness	operator know and follow the correct braking procedure?	things are captured and it can be identified whether the operator followed the proper braking procedure. Look for the last training, and also look for past operator performance and determine if he is a "top gun pilot."
Hazmat Awareness	Are there different procedures if a train is carrying hazmat?	What is the operator's training regarding Hazmat? Was he aware that there were 20 cars of flammable material? If so, are there different operating procedures? Look for training records on Hazmat.
Signal Awareness	At what point did the operator notice the defect signal?	Were there sensory or other issues that might have caused some delay?
Quick Thinking Ability	What was the Operator's ability to react to a disaster without panic?	Are these operators screened for psychological factors? Are they top gun pilots? Look for whether or not these employees are screened somehow.

The Lawyer's Job

In a civil case, a lawyer doesn't have to prove "reasonable doubt." All he or she must do is prove the "preponderance of the evidence."

It will be an easy job to plant in the brain of a jury any of these ideas. It would be all the easier if the railroad did an imperfect job of filing these training and work records. "Training records? What training records?"

In this case, it will be up to the railroad to prove that they did everything right.

The Rail Cars

Let's start with the basics. You know how everybody has communications, and cellphones, and screens and we're living in a golden age? The pace of technology has advanced so much, and things are so much better now?

Well, train cars are the opposite of that. Train cars are famous because they're basically the same as they were 100 years ago.

The Janney Coupler, which is the mechanism to attach the cars together was patented in 1897.

The Westinghouse air brake was patented in 1898 and is still the predominant way of stopping a train. Those air hoses that run from car to car are connected to a series of tanks, and a compressor in the engine provides compressed air that operates the brake mechanism. There are some more recent control system improvements, but basically it is the same as it has been for a century.

Is this a case of shark evolution? No, it's an example of an industry so big, and so old, that it's impossible to change it. The capital expense and general expense to retrofit the whole system to some new technology is cost-prohibitive.

Who Owns All of Those Railroad Cars?

Anybody can own a rail car. In fact, it's an interesting business proposition. The most common people who own rail cars are people who use rail cars all the time and need their own. Here is an example: Carbon black is a nasty material, so much so that the rail cars used to haul it are unusable for anything else. So, if you're a carbon black manufacturer, you might own your own rolling stock, just so you won't have to wait in line to ship your product.

That is not to say that the carbon black companies "need" to own their cars. They can just as well get into long-term lease agreements with someone who is in that business.

There is a link for Trinity Rail, who claims to be North America's largest rail car leasing company. According to their website, they own 140,000 rail cars. The railroads themselves, like Norfolk Southern, also own only about 54,000 rail cars. Trinity manufactures the cars in addition to leasing them out.

It's basically the same as truck leasing, and over the road trailer leasing. The leasing company gets to take non-cash tax write-offs (depreciation) and so there is a business in borrowing money, buying capital intense equipment, leasing the cars out, getting tax benefits, and collecting cash. It's a bit dependent on the overall economy, but there will be a need for their equipment for the foreseeable future.

Trinity Industries has done reasonably well as an investment. Here's the stock chart. Of course, they do similar things in other industries along with railroads.

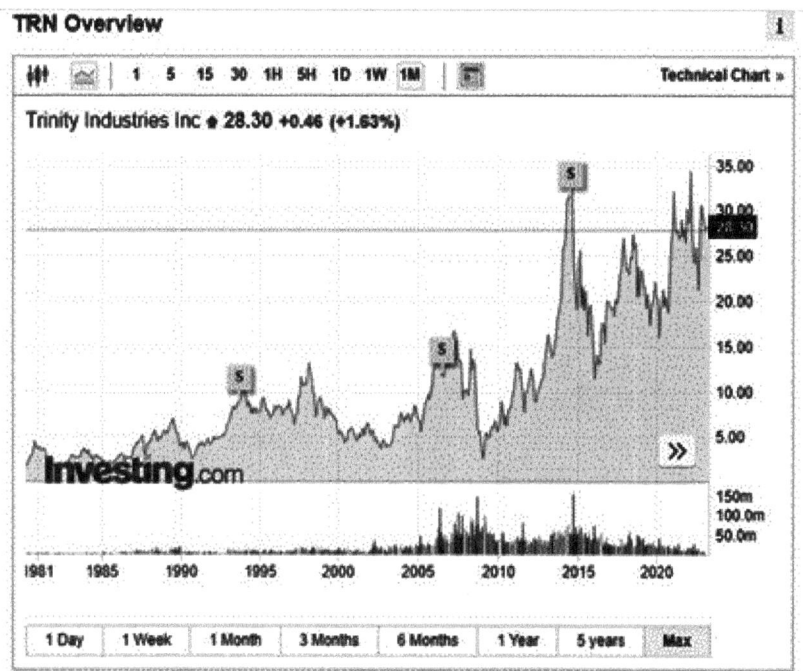

When a rail car breaks down, who fixes it? Well, there are people in that business too. Trinity has a network of rail car service facilities, and there are ways to get railway cars fixed if you need to.

Do these railroad cars ever get inspected?

There's a law that says that when a car is put into a train, it needs to be inspected by a "designated inspector." What does it take to be one of those? Well, for a few dollars, it seems that you, too can take a rail car inspection course. The pay is around $11 an hour.

Ultimately, it's the job of the train crew and/or the "carman" to inspect the railway cars before they're put onto the train. I put a link to a CSX carman in the Links and References. There are no educational requirements, but you have to pass the test, and have some welding aptitude.

The link to CFR215 is interesting. This is the law with regards to rail car inspection. It gives the inspection points and what to look for on a railroad car. It's basically cracks, breaks, failure points, and signs of overheating. Maybe you can visually inspect these things and see whether they're going to cause a problem.

Inspection Scenario

So, it's cold and dark, and they're putting a train together. There is an employee called a "car toad" that is supposed to do the work of inspecting the car, confirming no defects, and confirming that it's attached properly. This fellow is supposed to notice any cracks in the bearing housing, for example, see if there are any signs of overheating, or any other issues that might cause the car to be tagged out.

The Car Toad Dilemma

It's a federal requirement that he or she does his or her job. Is there objective evidence of this happening? At this point, the inspectors have a handheld device that captures the information.

There's pressure on the part of the boss for the employee not to tag out a car, and not to tag out too many cars. If an employee does this, it causes the railroad to have to do repair work and/or delay shipping. Do they want to do that? No. So, there is a built-in conflict of interest.

There's a case I've linked in the links and references where in a separate incident, the CSX railroad basically knowingly released bad cars into the world, a wreck ensued, and someone was injured. In that case, an employee who was zealously doing his job as a rail car inspector was chastised for doing too good of a job, and there was evidence.

Here's where we get back to the relationship between the Union and The Railroad, which we all know is "tense."

The Hot Box Car

I am much more interested in the boxcar with the hot box than the 20 cars worth of chemicals.

The railroad should be able to trace that thing back to the source, figure out who "inspected it" and when, and look at objective evidence that it was properly released.

Maybe.

All a lawyer would have to do is plant the seed of doubt in a jury as to whether this car was properly inspected.

This would be easier to do if the "inspector" was some kind of low wage employee that was in a dispute with management, some cold dark night in a railway yard in the Midwest.

An efficient lawyer would already know whether the railroad, Norfolk Southern, was involved in any other legal actions like the one below.

204

For that matter, the records for that car would be pulled, as well as maintenance records for all of the other cars on that railroad. Since railroad car technology has been around for a long time, some crafty lawyer and a statistician should know how many of these things are flunked in each week, systemwide, and be able to figure out whether a given inspection location was working properly.

And, as in the previous case, if it is found that there are flaws in the record-keeping system, that alone will have them screaming.

It's going to be up to the railroad to prove that their inspection system is effective, particularly at the location where our suspect car was added to the train.

Audit Trails

Here's a little table of potential audit trails that I, as an investigator, would start with.

Evidence	Line of Inquiry
Last inspector	Current training certificate, valid training certificate, eyesight, experience, working conditions at the time of the inspection, history of discipline issues, relationship with supervision and management
Inspection	Recent escapes, overall

System	system effectiveness, percentage of similar cars with inspection issues
Railroad Car Manufacturer	Similar defects and product issues, known defect
Repair Service	When is the last time this car needed repairs? Who did the repair? Could there be a repair failure
Railroad	History of whitewashing car inspections? Previous lawsuits?
Component Manufacturer	Similar defects in other railroad cars? History of
Railroad Car Owner	History of maintenance issues? Allowing cars to go beyond the recommended maintenance interval or rebuilding interval? Maintenance being done as required?

There is supposedly a role in this for the Federal Railroad Administration, but as we have indicated previously, the government is struggling to do this sort of thing right now. They can't do anything more than check a sampling.

There is an FRA database that is available to see how they're doing.

The Survivors

Now, it's time to look at some of the people involved at the scene of the wreck. We've already thought a bit about the hard-working train crew that was operating the equipment. We've also thought about the yard crew that was putting the train together.

Decisions are made by people, and not AI. They have baggage, and conflicting interests. There are different levels of experience, and different perspectives.

East Palestine Ohio

Let's start with this cold, dark, railroad town.

This place is so stereotypical of the post-industrial, post-agricultural small town that it was selected as a movie set about the topic.

The 2022 film "White Noise" included some of the townspeople as extras in a film about a big railroad disaster.

It's too small for their own Wal Mart, but there are two Dollar Generals. We usually can figure out what a town is about by counting the vape shops and dialysis places vs. the number of art galleries, but let's say that our preliminary search is heavily on the side of the vape shops.

The median income is $38K a year, and it's 98% white, for what that is worth. The little towns in the south like this have a bit of racial tension as well. The median income in the nation as of 2020 was about $73K.

This may or may not have made a difference in some of the decision-making processes, as the disaster unfolded. I am thinking about the evacuation decision, as well as the decision to do a "controlled burn" of one or more of the railroad cars full of vinyl chloride that was about to blow up.

2022 was a rough year for the football team, they were 1-8. The little town pecking order in this part of the country is heavily influenced by what kind of football team they have.

The Town Cop
The Chief of Police is linked in the links and references.

When the first call came out, it probably went to him. He was promoted to his job in 2017. He started as a part-time small-town cop in 1996, and over a period, worked himself up to being Chief.

It's a bit different in the north, but small-town cops in the south have in their experience "The Andy Griffith Show" from classic American TV. They imagine themselves to be like Andy, who is a revered figure in the community, but are always in danger of being Barney, who is a bumbling sideshow character.

The main job of a small-town cop in one of these places is to pull people out of the ditch that had too much to drink on Saturday night, and/or keep the local drug dealers under something that approaches control.

There is nothing in the resume or background on LinkedIn that suggests he paid attention in chemistry class. Let's say, for the sake of fiction, that he balanced congeniality and competence, and sufficiently navigated small town politics, but does not know much chemistry.

The Fire Chief

Let's say that the second call went out to the Fire Chief who also doubles as the Emergency Management person.

This fellow has a degree in Fire Services Administration and a master's degree in public administration from Columbia Southern University, which is in the lovely town of Orange Beach, Alabama.

He was with the Horry County SC fire department for 12 years and prior to that, had a stint in the Air Force. Despite the cold, he probably welcomed the small-town culture. He is originally from Darlington PA.

Horry County is where Myrtle Beach is and has a fairly big fire department. Let's say our fellow here was frustrated about his lack of upward mobility. He correctly took it on himself to get some more education. He "upgraded" to East Palestine, which is close to his old hometown.

Let's go out on a limb and say that he is well meaning and serious. He has seen a bit of chaos in his lifetime.

There is an investigation still going on about who authorized what and at what time. The story we are writing now is of the first few hours of the disaster. The Chief is thought to have eventually authorized the "controlled release." He may have had a chemistry class or two, and/or some hazardous materials experience. Maybe not. Another article says the non-chemistry-majors with the railroad hatched this plan.

The fire department in East Palestine was exhausted after all of this happened. They were the first to arrive and last to leave. Was this "heroic?" You, the reader may decide.

Does the part of him get played by Ben Affleck? Nah, you'd have to say not.

The Trainmaster
The trainmaster is the guy who picks up the phone when his frantic dispatcher says, "there's a train out of control."

There are no educational requirements, but you do have to have some tolerance for chaos. I've linked the job description.

First, the trainmaster is responsible for scheduling the crews. He keeps them legal from a consecutive hour standpoint, and keeps everything on time, you hope. It's stressful because the world is chaotic. It also helps to have experience as a locomotive operator, because you also need to investigate accidents like this one. You, the trainmaster, will have some help in this case because it has hit the headlines.

This guy probably lives where the nearest big railroad yard is. So, let's say he was at the end of the line, at the terminating point in PA.

It takes him awhile to get to the scene, but even so, he is the first investigator to arrive while the thing is an inferno.

The Safety Data Sheet.
This is the next question: Who knows what exploded and where it came from? In theory, there is a manifest for this train with that information that is stored somewhere other than the burning car.

With luck, someone produces the Safety Data Sheet for vinyl chloride. This one is from Airgas Inc.

On this safety data sheet, it says the following:

No action shall be taken involving any personal risk or
without suitable training. If it is
suspected that fumes are still present, the rescuer should
wear an appropriate mask or
self-contained breathing apparatus.

Airgas Safety Data Sheet

And, it also says:

Promptly isolate the scene by removing all persons from
the vicinity of the incident if
there is a fire. No action shall be taken involving any
personal risk or without suitable
training. Contact supplier immediately for specialist
advice. Move containers from fire
area if this can be done without risk. Use water spray to
keep fire-exposed containers

cool. If involved in fire, shut off flow immediately if it can
be done without risk. If this is
impossible, withdraw from area and allow fire to burn.
Fight fire from protected location
or maximum possible distance. Eliminate all ignition
sources if safe to do so

Airgas SDS

What, exactly, does it mean to be "trained" on this topic?
What this is, is an inoculation against a lawsuit. Someone
does something stupid, the producer says "sorry, we clearly
stated that only trained personnel should be messing with
this stuff, not our fault."

For a "large spill" it says to do this:

Immediately contact emergency personnel. Stop leak if
without risk. Use spark-proof
tools and explosion-proof equipment. Note: see Section 1
for emergency contact
information and Section 13 for waste disposal.

Airgas SDS

The Duty Officer

There is an 800 number for the plant, and an 866 number
for the 24-hour contact.

The first question is, do they pick up the phone?

Once they do, who answers? If it's midnight, the most
likely person is the plant superintendent. Most of the time

213

this is a management level employee that knows a lot about how to make the product, but no experience at all in disasters. Most of the big chemical plants have an assignment board that designates an emergency contact official that is "on duty" at night.

Is he or she supposed to be trained in this? No, he or she is an experienced plant employee but gets paid a lot not to spill it. The likely first reaction is for them to then call the plant safety manager. This is call number two.

In the meantime, the fire continues to burn.

The plant safety manager is called at 1 AM. Does he or she pick up the phone? Let's say, hypothetically, that he or she does. But they are not trained in this type of disaster either. It specifically says on the SDS not to mess with this stuff unless you are trained.

So now, you have to talk to some kind of corporate level safety person, which there probably is one of. Does he or she answer the phone? You're already on call number three, and it's 3 AM.

The Corporate Safety Officer

This may finally be someone helpful. He or she may have had experience in dealing with a mass gas leak of vinyl chloride.

There was a spillage of this stuff into a creek in New Jersey in 2012.

This story indicated that although terrible, no one died in that incident, although 20 people went to the hospital with breathing problems. What eventually happened was that the material diffused in the air (and water) and life sort of went on. But that is New Jersey.

214

The best idea at the time was to close the windows and keep away from it. A charcoal filter will take it out of the water.

First Responders NJ Protective Equipment

https://www.ishn.com/articles/96471-first-responders-failed-to-wear-respirators-in-vinyl-chloride-spill

An article in "Industrial Safety and Health News" says that over 700 people were eventually evacuated. The major problem was that the local fire department didn't have SCUBA equipment, and a lot of the first responders were severely affected.

What do you tell the Chief?

Are you, the corporate safety person, qualified to tell anybody what to do with a million pounds of burning vinyl chloride? Of course not. Nobody is. There were several other cars wrecked at the same time, with other chemicals, so the problem was more complicated than that. There are multiple phone calls, and multiple safety officials.

So, you tell the chief to get his people away from it and stand back. But the chief is correctly afraid that since the whole thing is under pressure, it's going to blow up. He probably didn't know about the previous leak, although the corporate safety person may have been aware of what happened.

He may or may not be aware of the other industrial disasters of history, and what the ramifications are. No two disasters are exactly alike.

Politicians, News People and Talking Heads

By dawn the next day, the politicians come out of the woodwork. The head of the Ohio EPA is on the news. The Governor has a press conference. There are helicopters overhead.

Who is in charge? Does the Chief get out his copy of the National Incident Management System quick reference? (I have linked it in the links and references) It tells you how to set up a command center to coordinate the response team.

Since he is trained in all of this, he should have had time to do a little incident planning exercise, and have figured out where to have this, and who is in charge ahead of time. Maybe by this time, with the fire still burning, he can address this. But in the meantime, he has bigger fish to fry. He is afraid his town is going to blow up.

By the afternoon, there are 75 jurisdictions, and there needs to be some decision coordination.

Decision Making Authority

The guidelines call for an "incident commander." But it doesn't say exactly who in the hell that is. Come to find out, there is an "incident commander" job description. The Type IV incident commander is for a complex situation, like this one, with multiple resources and jurisdictions. Is it the same as a hurricane "incident commander"? Anyway, our guy the Chief does not have time to ask a lot of questions. He coordinates the multiple fire departments and others, and because he is the local, the visiting emergency people defer to him temporarily.

At some point does incident command pass to a talking head or a politician? A very creative movie script can be written about this conversation, especially in this case.

Let's say hypothetically, that since Red Adair, the Patron Saint of Incident Response is not around anymore there may be a lively discussion on this topic.

The Amorphous They

At some point, this person enters. The Amorphous They is a person with authority, but no accountability. We talked about the Amorphous They earlier.

An airline pilot has both Authority and Accountability. Once he gets in the air, he is responsible for doing his job, and accountable for not doing it, 100%. He is licensed by the government for his ability to do this.

The guy at the window at your fast-food place has accountability, but no authority. If the order is screwed up, he is the one that catches hell. He is the most customer facing member of the system.

In a factory, a machine operator has minimal authority, and some, but not a lot of accountability. If he screws up a part or two, nothing bad happens usually. But this is not usually your highly motivated employee.

The plant manager of the same factory has more authority, and also more accountability. If some product gets out the door that is defective, he or she is accountable. He or she also has the authority to do something about it.

The Amorphous They may be some knowledgeable technical expert, or other person, that sits at the edge of the room. His, or hers, is that voice that says "Chief, you have to vent that rail car."

He or she has authority, but no accountability. This is like a white-collar criminal or a supervillain.

"They" thought it was a good idea at the time.

So that's how the "Amorphous They" works. The idea is thrown out. Several people in the room may have thought it at the same time, but only one says it aloud. No one is completely sure who said it.

When the story is told to a jury, later on, it's something like "Yeah, "they" thought it was a good idea to vent the rail cars to ambient to prevent an explosion, even though it may have caused a fish kill and multiple cases of lung irritation."

When the story is told later, no one can remember exactly who "they" were that had the idea. That way, sometimes, it's hard to determine who should be held accountable if the decision blows up literally in someone's face.

The "Amorphous They" make decisions all the time. There may be a cross-functional task force. There may be team meetings and donuts. "They" are making decisions based on one set of values, which may or may not be the openly stated values of the organization, such as it is.

So that's what happened.

The Aftermath

On February 6th, after some confusion about whether to evacuate the nearby area, "officials" made the decision to vent the remaining cars.

In this case "officials" would be the "Amorphous They."

The Wikipedia article, linked in the links and references, says that the cars were "vented" by "railroad personnel" using shape charges.

Do you want that job?

Once the material was "vented" and all of the fires were out, the cleanup could begin. There is ongoing disagreement on who was going to take the 1900 feet of contaminated railroad ballast, and all of that surrounding contaminated dirt. The Roadmaster, who is the railroad employee in charge of the track, only took a week to get the track to the point where the trains could run, and then he ended up tearing it out again because the EPA wanted to remove the contaminated soil.

Job security.

The Movie Scene

So, do you want to write the movie scene on this? The wreck burned for 3 days, controllably. You've had multiple conflicting orders on whether to evacuate the area. People are on the news whining about how they've been exposed to toxins. The situation is tense.

No humans died directly because of the wreck. 45,000 "animals" died, but they were fish. Maybe some of the local dogs and cats tragically passed away but there are no reports of mass livestock deaths.

Do you know or agree with who oversaw the response team? We know at first, it was blamed on the Chief, but now, sometime later, there may be a lack of agreement.

"Officials" made the decision to vent the cars, helped by the Amorphous They. It was done somehow, and it took weeks for the pieces to be picked up.

Multiple lawsuits have already been filed. But "They" won't be asked to take the stand. It'll be your hard-working small-town Fire Chief that will be on the stand.

← **Tweet**

Governor Mike DeWine ✔
@GovMikeDeWine   ...

Late this afternoon an @nscorp train derailed in Clark County. We don't believe hazardous materials were involved. @OhioEPA, @Ohio_EMA, & @OSHP are on scene supporting first responders. President Biden and Secretary Buttigieg called me to offer help from the federal government.

9:31 PM · Mar 4, 2023 · **197K** Views

More Wrecks

Oh, yeah. Since the time of this incident there have also been more wrecks on the Norfolk Southern line. This has the conspiracy theorists up in arms, but the reality is, there are more than 1000 train wrecks a year, and they don't always make the global news.

But like we said earlier, they are going to test the legal system because a clever lawyer for the plaintiff will say "see, these people don't know how to safely run a railroad."

Why People Don't Do Their Jobs—Train Wreck Version

Here is the list thus far, to the extent we can tell,

Employee/Person	Blame (High, Medium, Low)	Why They Didn't Do Their Job
Car Inspector	H	Ticked off and tired, adverse working conditions
Train Crew	H	Marginally trained, sleep deprived, probably ticked off due to recent Union stuff.
Railroad Car Owner	M	No one told them there was a problem, system to proactively inspect cars is weak.
Signal Inspector	H	Some question as to when the signal was inspected, may have been outsourced.
Town Cop	L	Nobody can be trained for this kind of disaster.
Town Fire Chief	L	Nobody can be trained for this kind of disaster. No training on what PVC is and why you should vent it, unaware of

		dangerous chemicals being hauled through town.
Chemical Company Emergency Spokesperson	L	Plenty of training in chemistry, probably imperfect knowledge of previous spills.
Amorphous They	M	No training and no accountability

Here You Have It

In a disaster like this, where there are many people and many complex systems involved, it is obvious that some of the people were more likely than others to have not done their jobs.

Or, as Murphy's Law of Uneven Distribution says, "When something hits the fan, it is not evenly distributed."

The only inevitability in this is the fact that because the system is what it is, another disaster is right around the corner, because people don't do their jobs.

Links and References

16 A Day in the Life of a Modern Auto Worker

For educational purposes, I want you to put yourself in the place of one of the hard-working people, in one of these big new highly automated auto assembly plants.

How do we know this stuff? Let's just say that we have connections.

It is useful for a few of the readers of this to understand who an auto worker is, and what his or her life is like. Think of it as cultural broadening.

Now, the hypothetical plant we're talking about is a big Korean assembly plant not too far from Atlanta.

11:30 AM, You hit the floor with a "Thud"

You're sleeping on your brother's couch. You're paying him $700 a month, which is half of his rent for an average, reasonably safe apartment in Lagrange. You fell onto the floor with a headache.

You're doing this because you're new on the job. You're not now and unlikely ever to be able to afford a little cookie cutter house in nearby Suburbia.

There is plenty of time to make it to work, since you're working the second shift, which runs from 3 to 11. Still, you've come in late twice in the last month, and they're threatening to fire you. There are distractions in your life.

You dig around in a pile of clothes on the floor to find your blue T-Shirt.

Life of a Temp

At a given time, in one of these places, anywhere between 10 and 30 percent of the workers are "temps" that is, "temporary employees". You don't work for the company; you work for a temp agency. Ironically, for the service of finding, background checking, drug screening, and giving you minimal training, the "company" gives them a fraction of your pay. There's no rule as to how long they're allowed to keep you as a "temp" either.

Does that make you angry yet?

Here's the other thing. It is very common for you to show up for your job and work shoulder-to-shoulder with someone who works for the "company" and gets more love and money. The "temp agency" is benefiting from your labor and minimizing the love.

The blue shirt designates you as a "temp". There are rules to the effect that a supervisor for the "company" is not supposed to boss you around. You have a "temp boss" to tell you what to do, and he also doesn't get as much money or love as a "company boss."

They issue you two of these on the first day, and nobody expects them to last more than a couple of months. Faded blue T-shirts are rare enough on the plant floor. No one stays around long enough for their shirts to get old.

You Need a Car

Time to go out and get into your car. You need a car to get to work, because there is no subsidized public transportation to the plant.

I guess you are proud of your car. It was bought with zero down from one of those little used car lots in town that you drive by all the time.

Let's say that you decided to get a "nice car" which is a used red car of some type with only 100,000 miles on it. You paid $7500 for it, which is a bargain, and they did you a favor by letting you finance it. Since you are a young person, you don't have $7500 saved up, so "they", namely the used car guy, gives you a break and finances the car.

"They" give you a 36-month loan, for 6.88% interest. Wasn't that nice of them? And you get to drive a red car.

Are you mad at this? No, not really, because you're unaware that "they" are taking advantage of you a bit. Your car payment is $227 a month.

You cruise into the QT.

Breakfast not at Tiffany's

You're driving 27 miles one way to work, and ironically, let's say that your car gets 27 MPG. You could have gotten a more practical model, but it wouldn't have been red.

You're using 2 gallons a day, at the current price of $3.25 a gallon, that means it's costing you $32.50 a week or $140 a month for transportation. But because you are who you are, you're paying another $100 a month for insurance, and depreciation is nowhere in here because in three years, when it is paid off, your car is going to have 150,000 miles on it. You're putting 14,000 miles a year on it, even if you park it on the weekends. It will start to break down. You will be late to work.

Are you angry yet? No, because you can't predict the future. You don't know what is happening to you yet. It's all part of A Day in Your Life as an Auto Worker

Here's your breakfast:

You don't eat this every day. Some days you have Hunt Brothers Pizza. Your lunch comes from the cafeteria at work and that is subsidized at least. A reasonable amount of food can be had for about $6. Let's be generous and say

that you drive through someplace on the way home, for another $7.00.

So, it costs you roughly $20 a day to eat. That's another $600 a month.

You get to the Plant

You have to wait behind the line of trucks. An endless stream of trucks is coming in and out of this place 24-7 and if you don't add an additional 10 minutes to your commute time, you end up being late.

You get to the parking lot. The salaried people get to park in the front, then the "employees." The "Temp" parking lot is in the back. You have to sprint to the door.

These big assembly plants are laid out in lines. There's a body line and a chassis line. You don't work on the line. You work as a material handler. Somewhere in the neighborhood of 50 percent of the headcount does nothing other than unpack boxes, put them onto a rack just right, and haul them to the line. There, either an employee or a robot grabs the component and installs it onto either the body or chassis. Toward the end, the two lines merge.

You are a material handler, just like 1000 other temps. Some days you pick components from the warehouse, sometimes you unbox them and load up the carts, and sometimes you just move things around.

It's easy work, but noisy, and dangerous. There are forklifts, and big cranes, and everything is gigantic but delicate. Most of the heavy lifting has been done away with. You've been there for a couple of months and have yet to see a car. The place is so big that all you see is the line. It's like Vegas too. There are no clocks. You can't tell what time it is.

In fact, the biggest enemy is boredom. It causes more quality and safety issues than anything else. Comically about every five minutes, they play the first 10 seconds of some famous song (Sweet Home Alabama?) (Don't Stop Believing?) Just when it wakes you up, and you want to dance along, they shut it off.

The night shift is terrible.

About you
Well, your typical new employee in a place like this is male, about 22, a bit too old for fast food but not really your world class workforce. About 20 percent of the workforce is female.

You are a product of the local school system, and you got your diploma. You didn't do well in math though. "Proficiency" in the local high school in Math is 22%.

Maybe you are an immigrant, and in this place, there could be a dozen languages being spoken.

For the moment we'll leave out the can of worms about the racial stuff, because it doesn't really matter.

You're all in about the same boat.

The Pyramid

There's one plant manager at the top of the Pyramid. You want to know something not funny? The average plant manager in the US automotive industry makes less than the franchisee at Chick Fil A.

Under him there may be a half dozen "process owners" that are the main authority figures. Engineering, Production, HR, Logistics, and Quality Assurance. There may be a layer under the production person for each line.

Below each of them there are several superintendents, high level technical experts, and senior people that gather data and make decisions. There may be some maintenance people who have specialized training.

From here on up in the pyramid it might be 15% of the workforce. These are the people that get paid enough to be a bit more comfortable.

Below them, there are the "lead operators." A few years ago, a lot of these companies figured out that having "line bosses" was unproductive and caused problems. So, you have a "lead person" that oversees your scheduling, communication, motivation, and they look over your shoulder to get you to do things right. The "lead operators" don't make that much more money than you do. They're technicians like you who have a little extra aptitude.

The Rest of You

Below them are you and the rest of the "associates." At any given time, the workforce may fluctuate between 10 and 30 percent "temps". Some people may be called in for a specific job. For example, there might be "sorting" where they bring in a crew for a few nights to go through a big box of nuts and bolts that got mixed up somehow.

The cost to train a new employee is estimated at up to 1-3 percent of the first year's wage. You're trained less than Chick Fil A employees, who get 2 weeks (4%) before their first "my pleasure."

The automotive people see no problem running an operation where the wages are low. The cost of this turnover is less than the cost of retaining employees by paying them more.

So that's the way it works. It's a lot like the rest of the system where the few people at the top are doing reasonably well, but everybody else is basically in the same boat.

What could possibly go wrong?

Getting back to you, the worker.

Since you are not good at math, let's lay this on you:

	Per Month
Gross Pay	$2,440
Taxes	$488
Net pay	$1,952
Auto Insurance	$100
Rent	$700
Car	$250
Gas	$140
Phone	$100
Food	$600
Expenses	$1,890
Net Disposable Income	$62
Disposable Income per Week	$16

We've been adding all of this up. With your 40-hour a week job, you have "disposable" income, after all of your expenses, about $16 a week. That's if you're a boy scout, and never go out for a beverage, and don't have any bad habits. And, if the price of gas doesn't go up too much more.

Of course, you could look for ways to cut down on your expenses we suppose. That's where you and 10 other people rent out a big house someplace and violate the R1 zoning until the neighbors complain.

You haven't had a disaster yet. Your car hasn't broken down, or needed tires, costing you money. Forget shopping for clothes. At least you have a blue shirt. So far, you haven't had any other bad luck. You also haven't approached the young female in the next line over for some

232

friendly fun. No telling where that could end up. She may already have a young one or two being watched by her mom.

Side Note

This article was originally written in November of 2023, when the price of gas was $3.25 per gallon, and there was presumed food inflation. The $16 could easily go to negative

There are a couple of other things.

No one told you when you took this job you literally would have nothing to show for it at the end of the month. That's if things go well. What they don't tell you if you are a temp, they can call you in the morning and tell you not to come in because the truck was late. Or, because there are too many of these cars in the world, they need to cut production.

So, if you lose one day's pay a month, you're breaking out the plastic.

We haven't talked about medical yet. If you're a temp, there is often some bad medical insurance that they will give you. But you'd better not get sick.

Are you angry yet? No, maybe you're just stressed out, and a bit burned out with nothing to show for it.

The Last Straw

You're driving through some little redneck town and some Barney Fife wannabe pulls you over for rolling through a stop sign. The cops give you a $300 ticket. Where is that money going to come from?

Now you're mad.

What they're not telling you.

At the prevailing starting wage of $15.25 an hour you may love your job, but it's basically a waste of time. In a way, you're better off crawling back into bed, and looking for something closer and better.

If you suck it up, and stay for a couple of months, and get your extra $0.50 per hour, you're looking at another $120 per month disposable income. Still no margin for error.

You're not going to eat a $9 sandwich at some nice little sandwich shop in Historic Lagrange. You're not going to buy a $150 pair of shoes at the shoe store. You won't buy a house in the new subdivision nearby. You might be able to move into your own place at some point, but you are very likely to end up worse off in a world of 9% inflation and 9% interest.

It is possible through some combination of hard work, cost cutting, understanding of math, and getting a side job, you might be able to hang in there long enough to become a "regular" employee at which time they treat you a little better.

There are side hustle opportunities sometimes. You could sell some of your fellow employees something that they would like, to help them through the night. Things like this have been known to happen.

Some of these places will train you to be a mechanic, or a robot programmer or quality guy, or process engineer. But you need to be good at math, remember? You could attempt college. That could be done in the hours between 8 and 11:30 but you didn't pay attention in high school.

According to the bureau of labor statistics, if you're a low wage worker, there's a 90 percent chance that you will still be stuck there 10 years later.

So that's your future. Sign you up, right?

Who wins?
So, in the grand scheme of things, in the big picture, who wins?

You know it's not you.

Your cousin, or brother, is putting up with subsidizing your rent. He is not winning.

The used car guy? Not really. He has a lot of customers trash their cars and walk away from his loans and he ends up holding the bag.

The Quick Trip or Dollar General? The person behind the counter gets paid less than you. It's possible that the stockholders of those companies are benefiting.

The car company? That's very questionable.

Does anyone else in the community benefit? It remains to be seen. We will listen to arguments either way.

Anyway, enjoy your night shift. We will listen to counterarguments if there are any. Bring your Links and References. We're trying to deal with the facts here, to the extent that we can.

17 The Island of Misfit Toys

One of the reasons people don't do their jobs is that they're in the wrong job. "Job fit" is an important topic. Most of the time, if a person is somewhere in the middle in personality type, and the job is somewhere in the middle with regard to the nature of the job, the workplace is functioning.

Market forces, such as they are, are also involved of course. The world needs a lot more people that can successfully install a toilet, compared to some occupation like nuclear physicist.

Historical Context

History is full of people that were failures in some boring job, but later became very famous at something else.

Here are some examples:

Person	Didn't do their job	Much better at their job
Albert Einstein	Lazy, incompe-tent patent clerk	Most famous nuclear physicist of all time.
Elvis Presley	Got a C in Choir at Tupelo HS,	Exceptionally talented musician and movie star

	movie usher	
US Grant	Failure at farming, shop keeping and finished near the bottom of his class at West Point	Winning general in US Civil war, President of the US (Not considered one of the better Presidents.)
Nicki Minaj	Rude server at Red Lobster	Celebrated award-winning Rapper
Walt Disney	Fired from his job at the KC Star for not being creative enough	Mayor of Disneyland
Mark Cuban	Fired from his low-level retail job for not opening	Founder of Dell and Shark Tank guy

	the store on time	
Madonna	Fired from her job at Dunkin Donuts for squirting customers with filling	International star plus billboard for why not to get plastic surgery

With a little research you can come up with a few more examples. It is much more common to have it go the other way, someone takes a temporary job and gets fired, and never makes it to stardom

https://www.youtube.com/watch?v=GvvGqkvZ-B4

Correct Job Fit
What we're talking about here is the correct job fit. Depending on the survey, somewhere between 11 and 14% of workers think that their current job fits their personality perfectly. This is at the same time only 32% of companies use personality tests for hiring.

The consequences of hiring a person whose personality does not fit their jobs are obvious, not the least of which is that it ticks them off. We talked about ticked off workers earlier.

So where is the disconnect? How do people get hired to jobs that don't fit their personality?

The Three Laws of Personality Matching
You can't always get paid for something that makes you happy.

Just because it makes you happy doesn't mean you're good at it.

It's common to look for a bad job to pay the bills

These are self-explanatory. We would all like to get by on talent, but that is a very hard thing to measure and determine.

Signs of Improper Job Fit
From the employee point of view, here are some signs that you've managed to get yourself into a job that doesn't "fit." Keep in mind that some jobs are inherently unrewarding, as we have said, and most of these factors may apply if you're in one of those.

I've linked an article about this topic from a certain point of view, because the writer has a bit of a one-sided view of "work." A lot of people have never scooped rock or finished concrete for a living. It makes sense from that point of view, because once an employee progresses into some kind of "career" these things apply. But the low wage workers don't usually have a "voice" nowadays.

You don't feel like you're making progress. If, in your job, you put forth effort, and you don't feel like you are progressing in your goals, the job might not be right for you. Alternatively, you, the employee, may need to rethink your goals.

You don't feel like you're taking advantage of your strengths. That implies that you know what your strengths are.

You aren't passionate about what you are doing anymore. There are a lot of "jobs" in the world that don't inspire passion, but people do them anyway, as Mike Rowe, the Dirty Jobs guy will tell you.

You aren't able to grow in your role. In many organizations, it is possible from the employee's point of view to make some job progress. In some, showing up for work consistently and doing well will lead you to become a lead person and ultimately move into management. But in a lot of places, such as any job for low wage workers, this is not the case and career advancement is rare.

Your values don't align with the organizations. We have seen examples of lack of organizational alignment, i.e. you're being asked to do something illegal. This is definitely a demotivator no matter what level of the organization you're in.

You have anxiety about heading to work each day.
Anxiety in and of itself is a sign of poor job fit.

Your relationship with your colleagues is shallow.
In many jobs, you're dependent on someone else in the organization to do their jobs so that you can. It requires collaboration and teamwork, and if you can't do that, it's a problem. If this consistently happens, the problem might be you.

You don't see a future in your organization. For low wage workers, the future may be "next week" but as I carried records from the basement of a big factory, into the back of a truck, to go to court, for a huge lawsuit, it was clear to me that the future might have been limited in that job.

You don't feel valued. People will work for a long time for little or no money if they feel valued, as we will find out when we examine volunteering.

Being yourself isn't possible. Certain jobs don't lend themselves well to being individualized, and if you value being yourself more than you value not working, you're probably going to have to change jobs.

You feel unstimulated in your role. As in the case above, certain types of work don't lend themselves to being stimulated. When it gets to the point where you can't tolerate this anymore, you're going to have to move on before Number 6 kicks in.

Santa's Elves

https://youtu.be/OuVcr-tXm-A?si=Sz614KQCYoAMO5ca

This video, from the TV special, which is now nearly 60 years old, sums this up perfectly. You would have to say in this case that the supervisor is engaged, although a bit abusive. He chastises his employees in front of the whole team and has low tolerance for employee individualism.

Possibly all 11 of the above items apply to this fellow. In the world of TV, he eventually goes on to become a hero. But that works on TV better than it does in real life. He is just as likely to not do his job, and spill paint, and paint his little wagon poorly.

Personality Testing

We touched on this awhile back. The basic concept is that if you, the employer, have a way to screen for personality, you can improve the likelihood that your employee will fit into his or her job.

There are several drawbacks to this:

It is expensive. If you're hiring someone who is going to be loading boxes into the back of a truck you may or may not care what their score is on the Myers Briggs test.

It gives you unreliable results. If a candidate is smart, they will fill out their personality survey based on what they think the company wants to hear, rather than what their actual personality is.

It gives cookie-cutter results. If you want to fill your organization with drones that think a certain way, this is a possible method. However, this is not altogether a great idea. It leads to poor decision making and leads to people not doing their jobs.

It's possibly illegal. There are some aspects of personality that may be culturally or biologically rooted; therefore, some elements of personality may be considered a medical condition. Example: "Over the course of a day do you experience many mood changes?"

Do you know what's even worse than personality screening? Having an interviewer try to guess the personality of the candidate by some physical characteristic, or accent, or some other non-job-related aspect of the candidate's lives.

That is the definition of discrimination and will lead the interviewer into a lot of hot water.

Why People Don't Do Their Jobs: Job Fit

There is a lot in this, and it leads to a lot of other areas of consideration.

Hiring strategy should be a conscious management decision. One alternative is to hire whoever you can, for as cheaply as possible, and not be surprised if they quit and/or do a crappy job. In some jobs that works.

That's why temporary services companies were invented.

There's another strategy that says that when you're hired, from the point of view of management, the company wants you around forever. Therefore, they're going to take a lot of time and energy to screen you, train you, motivate you and presumably have higher expectations. If that's the case they're going to also expect you to have a personality such that you will fit into their work group, don't tick people off, and do your job, and hopefully, take a little initiative.

There are other strategies, enough so that yet another book can, and should, be written on this because there has been some evolution of this through the years. We have already experienced a day in the life of a baggage handler and auto worker.

This problem will never go away, because it is endemic to the human condition. It also is dependent on economic conditions at a certain time period, and the fact that people will suck it up and do a job even if it doesn't fit their personality in order not to starve.

That's why lack of job fit will always be a reason that people don't do their jobs, as your rude, inefficient waiter Nicki Minaj will tell you.

244

PS: You know what's even worse?

Someone that thinks they're going to be the next Nicki Minaj, and some dimwit Red Lobster manager makes the mistake of hiring them into a customer service role. They will not do their job, tick off the customers, and cause a lot of problems.

But obviously, there is a very small but greater than zero chance that from the point of view of the worker, it'll work. They are "sure" they will be famous at some point. They might be the one in a million.

Ironically, it's a lot of work to be famous, as Nicki herself will probably tell you. You must rehearse, practice, hire people to shoot your videos and record your stuff, and at the end of the day, there is some other little Nicki Minaj wannabe that is ready to take your job. I have a link in the links and references. Makeup and hair are time consuming.

Plus, the hours are bad. Being famous is work.

We haven't talked about "talent" much, because it is very rare, and you will often find that these "talented" people are very hard working. At a very minimum, they must work out constantly to keep from being flabby.

Reportedly Mick Jagger, who is 80, stays in the kind of shape he is in by constant diet monitoring, and traveling with two semi-trucks full of exercise equipment.

Taylor Swift gets up at 7 AM, works out, does songwriting and other grunt tasks, gets transported somewhere to be interviewed, and in the last three months of the year is doing 30 concerts in 15 cities.

Plus, she is expected to stay out all night, have selfies taken with her fans, and do other forms of self-promotion. Most normal people would not put up with all of that.

But these people are committed to their jobs, so they don't make it seem like work. The probability that someone is rude and lazy is going to be famous is just high enough to keep people trying it.

Links and References

18 Don't Ask Me, I'm Just a Temp

Temporary workers are increasingly common in the economy, and there is some evidence that they are less likely than "real" workers to do their jobs.

Being a temp, in and of itself, is not a direct reason for people not doing their jobs. In fact, temps are sometimes more likely to do their jobs than your actual employees. But a lot of temps have a lot of the issues we've talked about already.

As usual, there are stories.

Let's define the term first

Definition of "Temps."

Well, according to the US Chamber of Commerce, a temporary employee is someone employed "at will" for a short time so that you can get some work done.

A "Temp" can either work directly for an organization or for a "staffing agency."

I used to do that. One summer I worked for a place called "Help Incorporated." If a business needed a few grunts for one reason or another, they would call the office, and the office would send out some people. The jobs were difficult, very often dirty, and since it was the middle of the country, a lot of it was food related. Example: I once cleaned out the freezer in a big factory that made TV Dinners, because the freezer had broken down. It was July, so there was an element of fun to it since they issued a coat to us when we showed up.

My brother used to call it "Hell Incorporated" which was not all that funny.

Several of my clients now are in this exact sort of business.

A "Temporary" employee is different than a "contract employee," in that a contract employee may be an independent contractor, or LLC. I am a "contract employee" for a few companies around here right this minute, as a matter of fact. There are some legal nuances that make it important to know the difference.

Temporary or contract employees differ from "outsourcing," which we will talk about in a later chapter, in that in "outsourcing" the company you contract to is contracted to do a job, and it is up to the outsource company to figure out how to do it.

https://youtu.be/JHoMRdYus00

Who are the Temps?
According to Zip Recruiter, the temps around me, in Atlanta, are making on average $14.86 per hour or slightly less than the $18 per hour that the people at Wal-Mart get.

So, they're low wage workers. There was a chapter about them earlier.

Benefits of using Temps (From the Organization's point of view)
Well, since I am a former temp myself, and have been around a little, I am practically authoritative on this from the point of view of the organization. Here are some benefits to use of temps:

Staffing Flexibility
Like the above example, if you need a few fellows to do some very temporary job to solve some very temporary

problem, temps are perfect. You, the organization, can do the project and release the workers back into the environment to return the next time.

Cost Savings
Along with flexibility is the idea that you don't have to assign one of your "world class" employees to do a given activity that doesn't require "world class skill." Example: The automotive people have an activity called "sorting" where you go through a huge bin of nuts and bolts that were mixed up. It doesn't take a highly paid experienced worker to do that.

Specialized Skills
Right now, I am thinking about "disaster recovery." There are some specialized "disaster recovery" activities, and it is possible that you can call up your temporary recruiter, and get a particular job done.

The more obvious example is a service like Fiverr or Upwork, who I could hire to temporarily edit this book, for example. This is good for jobs that can be done remotely.

Reduced Recruitment Time
Examples: a freezer full of rotting TV dinners. A railroad car full of lettuce that was stuck on a siding somewhere. A concrete company that couldn't get the concrete truck far enough up into a driveway and had to use wheelbarrows to pour the whole thing. All you need to do is make a call (if you're lucky). The customers use a temp service if they need human power quickly.

It helps to give the temp service a little more notice, however.

Trial Period for Permanent Positions

I see this quite a bit. Some companies use "temps" to try out a prospective employee. If the "temp" is reliable, and okay around the place, they may receive an offer for an entry-level full-time job.

There are limits as to how long someone can be a "temp" however, from a liability standpoint. The US Department of Labor thinks it's one year, but I have been in places where people have been "temps" for much longer. There are legal and moral objections to that, however, so it is a risky strategy.

Drawbacks of the Use of Temps--Limited Training and Familiarity:

This one is fairly self-explanatory in that you don't need any specific training in the fine art of moving wet concrete around in a wheelbarrow. But it does take a little balance and dexterity, so it is not for everybody.

In a general way, the organization that uses these temps needs to keep an eye on them if the job is more complex or requires a little more training.

Otherwise, they won't do their jobs.

Inconsistent Workforce

That much is true. When we showed up in the morning there was a big smoke-filled room with steel folding chairs, and whosever butt was in that seat in the morning got the assignment. A significant fraction of the workforce was what we used to call "derelicts" and it was not uncommon for them to work for a day or two to get enough money for their lifestyle and then disappear.

So, from the customer's point of view, any sort of training was good only for the length of time that guy showed up.

A lot of these guys had "lifestyle issues" as we now say.

Lower Commitment to Quality
This can also be a bit of a drawback. In an earlier chapter we talked about employees who were removed from any kind of authority and/or customer accountability. So, if the job was such that quality was an issue, the people I worked for were mindful of that.

In fact, I would show up for a job, and I could tell that the customers were a bit suspicious. They had evidently had some mixed experiences.

I will say, though, in several of the temporary employment companies that I work for now, there are quality metrics, and the quality of the work of the temps is comparable if not better than the regular workforce.

So, this issue can be managed with some effort.

Communication Challenges
This is also a bit of an issue, not only because a lot of these employees are immigrants, but a lot of them are not technically sophisticated. Most of the workplaces I go into have terminology and internal designations for things, and in these cases, there is danger that the temp won't have any idea what you are talking about, and therefore not do his or her job.

Lack of Accountability
Temporary workers might feel less accountable for the long-term consequences of their work, which could impact their attention to detail and commitment to quality. The

temporary nature of their employment may reduce their motivation to invest in quality outcomes.

Transition and Handover Issues

I can see this being a bit of an issue in a medical or other technical operation, where the day is over, the temp says, "see ya later" and the day shift comes in and has no idea what went on.

Most of the time this can be managed by supervision doing its job, since there should be some sort of protocol to capture that information on a regular shift change situation.

Dependency on External Agencies

This is another thing. How much of your labor force do you want to commit to be the type of low wage worker? These employees could get ticked off, disengaged, not show up, need to be constantly retrained, and in a general way, are temporary.

A trained, effective workforce is an asset of the company and can give you organizational continuity.

From the Standpoint of the Employee

Usually, the employee is aware of the pros and cons. In my case, as a summer job to make a few dollars, it was fine. It would have been less fine if I had dependents and expenses over and above.

Transportation is a bit of an issue. One of the things they would do is give you an address, and in those days, there was no GPS, and we, the workers, were normally expected to find the job. The assumption was that I had a car, and the expense of this was borne by me.

Safety: Well aside from the day I carried scrap car batteries into the back of a truck, the worst day was in a place that did metal reclaim.

There was a big chopper, about two stories tall, and a crane. My brother and I were the temps, a third guy who was a permanent employee that we knew from school, was "training us."

A huge piece of equipment scooped up a scoop full of diesel engine blocks, which were ground up into chunks. A door would open, and these irregular hunks of metal would tumble down the belt. Our job was to sort it, magnetic, non-magnetic, and "pot metal" and throw the chunks off the belt and into a pile. We stood on a catwalk, about six feet off the ground.

But the sides of the belt were low and every so often one of these huge pieces of metal, 60 pounds or more, would tumble down the platform. where we were sorting. We were expected to be agile and alert enough not to get hit. There was no safety stop on the belt, there was no such thing as a hard hat. I had steel toed shoes, but that was not mandatory, and there was no ear protection.

There is a study cited below to the effect that in addition to temps being hurt on the job more than regular employees, their perception of whether something was "dangerous" or not was completely different, hence the example we had here.

The Worst Example of This in History
After the Chernobyl Nuclear Disaster in 1986, it took 350,000 people to take part in the cleanup. These were mainly current or ex members of the Russian army, who were "volunteered" to scoop up the nuclear dirt.

According to the article I linked, the "authorities" didn't know or tell the workers what they were scooping, and there was a two-minute time limit for an employee to run onto the roof, do some cleanup, and run off before they got their limit of radiation exposure.

Permatemping and other Perils

There's an interesting survey of temporary employees from the National Employment Law Project, in the links. This survey pretty much echoes some of the things we've talked about here: "Permatemping," poverty level pay, wage theft, and safety concerns are consistent with my experience on this.

There is also some management retaliation if the temp makes any sort of attempt to complain about any of this.

Temps

In a general way, is it a good or bad thing to have temps, from the perspective of trying to get people to do their jobs?

My opinion is that the use of temps is just like the use of other types of employees. If the temps are drunk, ticked off, disengaged low wage workers who have no accountability, they're probably not going to do their jobs.

If they're well supervised, selected with some care, trained on the job, the job and processes are well thought out so that the temp can do them, and you have alarm systems in place to warn you if there is a problem, then you're probably good.

A calculation should be made as to what the cost of failure would be and adjust the expectation backward into the decision of whether to use temps. Example: The airline doesn't hesitate to use temps and outsourcing to handle baggage, which is lower risk, versus doing maintenance on the aircraft.

Links and References

19 Doubtsourcing

Doubtsourcing ls like outsourcing, but not really.

We discussed temps in the previous chapter. Outsourcing is where you decide to farm out some activity to an organization that is better at it than you are, or what you aspire to be. There are some similarities between temps and contract employees in that they are not part of your permanent organization.

Outsourcing has gone on for a long time.

Machiavelli on Outsourcing
Here are some quotes:

Mercenaries and auxiliaries are useless and dangerous; and if one holds his state based on these arms, he will stand neither firm nor safe; for they are disunited, ambitious, and without discipline, unfaithful, valiant before friends, cowardly before enemies; they have neither the fear of God nor fidelity to men, and destruction is deferred only so long as the attack is; for in peace, one is robbed by them, and in war by the enemy.

The mercenary captains are either capable men or they are not; if they are, you cannot trust them, because they always aspire to their own greatness, either by oppressing you, who are their master, or others contrary to your intentions; but if the captain is not skillful, you are ruined in the usual way.

Niccolò Machiavelli "The Prince" 1513

So, the greatest management consultant of all time, who had a lot of experience with people not doing their jobs, was down on the idea.

Outsourcing Failure

On December 24, 1776, a detachment of mercenaries, the Hessians, had tied on a good Christmas Eve drunk in Trenton NJ, allowing an undersized, poorly equipped force led by George Washington to sneak up on them and take the town with minimal bloodshed.

In short, people didn't do their jobs. We can have the conversation as to whether they were considered outsourcing or temps.

The workforce was doubtsourced, and drunk, disengaged and in all likelihood ticked off, since being ticked off is a natural state of consciousness for Hessians.

The alarm broke down. Either the guards were asleep at their posts, or they sounded the alarm, and no one responded.

The King of England, who was in charge of all of this, did not do his job. He, and his mediocre General Howe, thought that this outsourcing organization would be effective. Since presumably Machiavelli was part of his princely training, King George knew, or should have known, that mercenaries are helpless. He therefore exhibited two of the classic definitions of Entrenched Mediocrity:

The organization accepts mediocrity to avoid the cost of change

A widely known problem is allowed to continue despite obvious risk

Outsourcing Examples

In the industrial setting these things are fairly common because there are some nuanced processes that are messy, require some expertise, or are so annoying that they detract from the overall purpose of the business, which is to make stuff and sell it.

Here are some examples:

Activity	Description	Outsourcing Rationale
Powder Coating	Very high-quality paint, applied electrostatically	Finicky process, requires a lot of upfront investment and employee training
Electroplat-ing	Ref: Chrome Plating, used to adhere a metal coating to a surface. Used in power transmission and in electronics.	Requires a lot of nasty chemicals, there are disposal and waste management issues
Wastewater	Wastewater often needs to be	Needs to be managed

treatment	treated before being discharged.	professionally to avoid being shut down by the EPA.
Industrial Gasses	Supplier-owned distribution and storage of gasses like nitrogen and oxygen.	Suppliers are happy to pay for storage equipment, which is convenient for both.
Construc-tion	Turnaround construction and other types of construction management.	Depending on the equipment, outsourcing entity can be better equipped and have more experience in this area.
Calibration	Monitor calipers, gauges and other measuring equipment.	Internal employees lack measuring device expertise and would rather focus on doing their jobs.
Material Handling	Forklift drivers and others hauling supplies. to the assembly line (Automotive)	Reduce "permanent" headcount, cost reduction vs. "world class workforce."
COTS item	Storage cage for	By focusing on this

cage.	nuts, bolts and sundry items, often run by Grainger or one of those similar supply houses.	area, there is better organization, fewer lost items, and control of inventory for various components. Convenient for the material handlers.

The best forms of outsourcing are in cases where there is specialized equipment or expertise that the outsourcing entity can develop, allowing them to focus on certain aspects of the process, allowing more efficient operations and problem solving.

Here are some examples from the post-industrial economy.

Activity	Description	Outsourcing Rationale
IT Outsourcing (Hardware)	Installations, Equipment repair, replacement	Outsourcing entities can focus and be better at this (Common for Government operations)
IT Outsourcing	Software	Expertise,

(Software)	management and installation, "Help Desk" activity. IT Backup, Server services, internet services.	focus on these activities, increased reliability and reduced cost.
Janitorial Service	Clean the place up, at the convenience of the organization.	Lower cost and better reliability than hiring in-house janitors. Also common in government. You don't have to hire and administer low wage employees.
HR Management	Administers benefits and paychecks, monitors HR issues, maintains training records.	Ref: ADP and others who have higher accuracy than hiring someone internally to manage.

The need for specialized expertise, and desirability of some organizations not to hire a lot of nerds has led to a major outsourcing industry springing up.

A major user of this type of outsourcing is the US Government, who very often does outsourcing for specific tasks that are outside the focus of the organization. Example: When someone with the Social Security Administration has his or her laptop break down, who do you think fixes it? The government has found out that it is faster and cheaper to ship it overnight to an outside entity, have it repaired, and returned the following day, rather than fill out whatever requisitions or other overhead activity that it takes to do this.

https://youtu.be/TRN4oSIzCvY

The same thing is true for major corporations that have a lot of IT infrastructure.

I know of a company that specializes in IT installation in hospitals. When a hospital needs to upgrade their IT system these are the employees that crawl around in the ceiling and run cables. By focusing on this specific industry this client has developed specialized expertise, is used to a hospital environment, and can do the job much faster and better than the hospital could by hiring and training outside employees.

So, these are the good stories. There are a few that are not so good.

The $1 Million Freezer

According to a recent news report, a janitorial service was working at Rensselaer Polytechnic Institute. This service, in upstate New York, is being sued because one of its employees flipped the circuit breaker. This shut up an annoying alarm.

The alarm was attached to a freezer, which housed a 20-yearlong research experiment. The lawsuit is for more than $1 million in costs associated with the lost research.

According to the report, when the event happened, the researchers did a risk analysis. They somehow determined that the freezer could be kept running. A possible contributing side factor is the fact that they had to wait for a manufacturer's technical service person to schedule a repair.

They posted a variety of signs on the freezer to the effect of "yes, we know the alarm on this freezer is annoying but please don't shut it off."

The janitor, working for Daigle Cleaning Systems, an outsourcing entity, ignored the signs, flipped a circuit breaker, and shut off the alarm and everything else, compromising the experiment.

The Major Problem with Doubtsourcing

It's communication. This is a perfect example. The information did not reach the janitor on the floor at the time. There is no telling how close it ever made it. There is a natural communication barrier between the outsourcing entity and "the organization."

In this case, It is possible that if the supervision for the cleaning service sat down with the engineers, and brought in the cleaners, and said "whatever you do, don't shut this freezer off" that would have been better. It wouldn't have been foolproof though. Some people don't understand spoken English either.

A clever lawyer would look for training records to this effect, and then say "see, you, the "plaintiff" didn't adequately train or communicate to anybody. You just put up a few signs and called it good.

The lawsuits are going to fly on this one, and it looks to me like the cleaning service does have some defense. Communication processes may have been ineffective.

A "reasonable jury" might conclude that despite the signage, the University didn't sufficiently communicate this to the cleaning service, particularly in light of the lack of a requirement to read English, if there is a lack of requirements.

But that doesn't help the situation regarding the poor lab test. Twenty years of research down the drain. I hope it didn't have a cure for cancer in it.

I, a quality-systems professional, could be an expert witness in this case. You know where to find me.

The Importance of Records

This is a side point, because documentation of all of this is going to be critical.

The contract between the cleaning service and the University will be evidence. It will have a job description, and in it, the minimal qualifications for an employee to work in this outsourcing service, which might be to be able to read and understand instructions written in English.

If there are written training records on either the outsourced cleaning people or the decision to temporarily allow the freezer to run, that will be important.

Why People Don't Do Their Jobs: The $1 Million Freezer

There was a freezer malfunction. This was a 20-year-old freezer, which is a long time for a freezer, but maybe a proactive upgrade would have solved the problem.

Alarm system failure: There needed to be a management decision about what to do if the alarm goes off. This should be thought of when the alarm is installed and documented.

The behavior of "support personnel" was ineffective. Once that management decision is made, if it affects the behavior of "support personnel" make sure everybody in the system is aware of the fix, and do training, and retain training records. Sticky notes and temporary instructions are not really very good means of communication.

Employees are undertrained. Extend training into the outsourcing organization. Many outsourcing organizations have a training function that does this very thing.

In addition to that, since this is an outsource situation, someone needed to make sure communication ability is a job qualification and keep records of that too. Also, retain employee hiring records to confirm that the employees were properly screened before working in this area. This is a job for supervision, and we will address that activity later.

We'd first hope that the problem never happens, and the system works.

If the system doesn't work, we will want to know what the story was, and that's why the records are critical.

Another Drawback: It Ticks People Off

There is another drawback to outsourcing, in that unless done carefully, it has a chance to tick off the regular workforce.

As we saw earlier, a ticked-off workforce is yet another reason for people not doing their jobs.

The regular workers may believe that the company doesn't respect them. It further suggests that their own jobs were at risk, and ultimately, the quality of their work will be negatively affected.

Unions dislike the whole idea because it represents a reduction in bargaining power.

There is a research paper I have linked in the references to the effect that in organizations that use outsourcing, the wages of the current employees go up more slowly. So, the evidence is that they have a point.

Doubtsourcing Success Story

This is an interesting story. There is a company, RJ Corman, in Nicholasville Kentucky, that started with one high school graduate with a backhoe and evolved into a very impressive nationwide "railroad services" company.

The story is, there was some kind of local railroad issue, the "regular employees" didn't do their jobs, and this fellow, RJ Corman, just barely out of high school, appeared on the scene with his backhoe.

He became known for promptness and efficiency, and gradually became the preferred outsourcing organization for fixing railroad derailments. This fellow eventually evolved to a huge business with 1400 employees, a personal train, a helicopter and he eventually started running short line railroads, materials handling, logistics, and a lot of other railroad-related activities.

Did this tick anyone off? Well, it is possible that he ticked off the unions, the permanent employees that he replaced, and any number of competitors, but at the end was rewarded for doing his job. That would make him a top gun pilot with a backhoe.

He became known as the "Railroad Red Adair."

Speaking of Red Adair

This fellow was so famed in the practice of oilwell firefighting that a movie was made about him. He got his start by basically singlehandedly approaching a burning oil well with a wrench and shutting it in by hand.

Later, he innovatively developed various methods for shutting off oilfield blowouts and was hired to shut off a lot of those oilwell fires during the Iraq War. He became rich and famous for his ability to cope with disaster.

Here's a quote:

"They've been to school, but they haven't been out bustin' their asses on oil rigs," he told Singerman. "Arguing with an engineer is like wrestling with a pig. Everybody gets covered with crap, and the pig's the only one who has a good time."

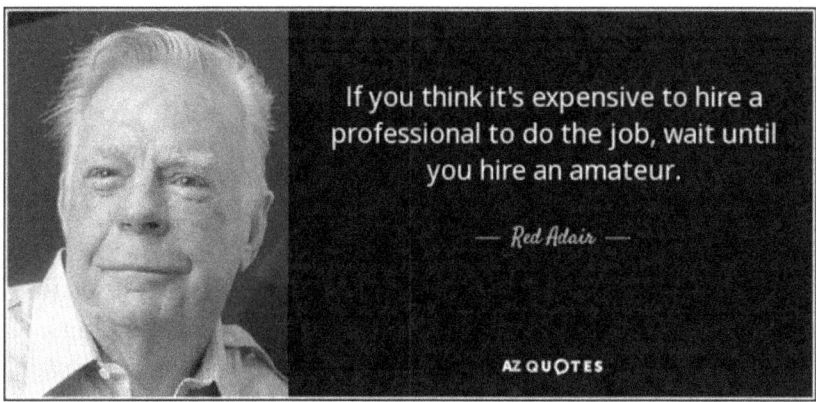

If you think it's expensive to hire a professional to do the job, wait until you hire an amateur.

— Red Adair —

AZ QUOTES

Thought Question

Would Halliburton, or Schlumberger, or any of those other giant oilfield companies be better off hiring Red as a full-time employee? The answer is that we'll never know. It depends on the size of the company and the tolerance of the company to pay this fellow's salary between fires.

Also, in my opinion, Red would have never been hired. I am going to go out on a limb and say that our man Red would not have been a pleasant person to have around the office and would not have necessarily looked good in a suit. He might have had his own reality show if he was around today. Maybe, in a way, that's another important consideration. Red must have been another Top Gun Pilot.

He was extraordinarily gifted in an unusual field where people would spend large amounts of money to solve a problem. Not all outsourcing entities are that gifted, and it is a business calculation as to whether a given operation can or should be farmed out.

Doubtsourcing: What to Make of All Of this?

Well, here is my opinion on this, after having worked for, around, and with a variety of these entities:

For a defined purpose, and limited scope, if the work is properly planned and communicated, outsourcing is fine.

When the work is poorly communicated, not monitored properly, and when the outsourcing organization gets filled with low wage employees, it is less fine, and becomes just as bad as the workers they are replacing. Outsourcing sometimes brings in employees who are just as impaired, poorly trained, and ticked off as those of the parent organization, but to that, you can add even less accountability.

It is common for outsourcing entities not to do their jobs. It is possible that any cost savings, or reduction in organizational complexity will be offset by some kind of screwup.

But for some problems outsourcing is the preferred option.

Why People Don't Do Their Jobs

Links and References

20 Lessons from Volunteering

Food Gatherers in Ann Arbor, Michigan, is a "food rescue" operation that has as its mission to alleviate hunger and its causes in its community.

This organization was founded in 1988 by the owners of Zingerman's Deli, which is a very famous deli not too far from the U of Michigan.

This organization has an annual budget of $15M and a workforce of 30 full and part-time staff doing the important job of collecting food from various sources and distributing it to local charities and distribution centers in the local community.

The reason I am putting this story in a book about why people don't do their jobs is because this is just the opposite. This organization is doing its job. Also, they are doing so with the help of 2800 volunteers, and a very well-equipped building in Ann Arbor. I would say that if there is a mission, people don't mind doing their jobs even if they don't get any pay.

Emotional rewards are sometimes enough.

The Profit Motive and Performance
This is an important question: What is the overall performance of a non-profit organization relative to a for-profit activity.

There are several academic studies on this topic. The most interesting are related to hospitals, namely, can a non-profit organization provide better quality care, measured in various ways, compared to the for-profit hospitals.

In most of the cases, the non-profits have significantly better performance and have better patient success rate, compared to a hospital that is interested in quick patent turnaround and capacity utilization.

It's estimated that one out of eight families in Ann Arbor, one of the most prosperous places in Michigan, are "food insecure." We have talked about some of these people earlier as well.

What is the Value?

The purpose of management is to maximize the wealth of the shareholders. In a case like this, a non-profit which does have shareholders but is not interested in profits, how would you "value" the organization? How would you know that the management structure and directors were doing their jobs?

Well, the people that do this sort of thing have a lot of non-financial measurements of success. The main ones of these are mission impact, stakeholder satisfaction, program stability, and long-term viability.

The most recent annual report from Food Gatherers says that the organization provided more than 6 million meals in the local area, and distributed 7 million pounds of food. This organization also receives food from government sources, and because of its financial strength is able to buy and distribute food as well by purchasing food in bulk.

https://youtu.be/9BzB8jjhEtg

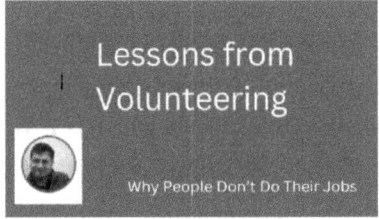

Lessons from Volunteering

We have talked about the "corporate mission" at several points throughout this work of literature. This is not especially well thought out in a lot of businesses. According to a study I have linked in the Links and References, 92% of companies can come up with something that approaches a statement of "core values" but this is poorly communicated throughout the organization.

A company with "values" is thought to be able to recruit better employees, have a better brand image, and have higher employee satisfaction.

In a for-profit organization this will totally backfire if it later comes to light that the core values are all about the piece of paper, and the management uses this to manipulate the employees psychologically.

276

Here are some lessons from volunteering that might be useful to some for-profit organization where people are not doing their jobs.

Be Nice.

There are up to 2800 volunteers, and 80% of the hours worked are by a core group of consistent volunteers. It is in the culture of the organization to treat these people respectfully.

The typical volunteer digs through a big box of expired fruit and/or canned goods for a reason. They have a sense of duty. The organization surveys their volunteers on an ongoing basis and attracts people who want to have a sense of belonging to the community. Some need to fulfill various volunteer requirements, and some have court-mandated community service.

Whatever their motivation, it makes sense to give the people that volunteer a positive experience, and that includes being nice to them.

Have the place organized.

A lot of thought has been given to having the plant layout well organized and meeting the Safe SERV requirements for food handling.

This includes having the workstations set up to sort through the food properly, there is an engineered workflow of food into and out of the place, and the roles of the volunteers in the main shop are clearly defined.

What that means is that when someone shows up for their volunteer shift, they can expect to work on the mission, rather than wait for the crew to get organized.

Volunteers like instructions.

In a sense, this is an efficient production operation, and is a bit complex for someone that is not from that line of work. The volunteers want to be there and want to feel like they are contributing.

So, they don't mind a little direct communication, and appreciate being told clearly what to do. This is slightly different from "barking out orders" but the point is, that the work instructions are clear enough that someone off the street can do them with minimal training.

Have a Variety of Jobs

Your typical factory assembly line has a workforce that is screened to lift at least 35 pounds, and not have impairments. The volunteer situation can't be that picky. They are welcoming all walks of life, and all sorts of physical conditions.

Therefore, they need to have a variety of jobs that have different types of skills and abilities. Since there is no pay, no one worries about who works faster or harder than anyone else. They want to contribute their time in whatever way they can.

A volunteer organization like this attracts people in the first place that are of a certain personality who are a bit more accepting.

Schedule predictably

We talked earlier about a workforce that has obligations outside of the organization, such as child and elderly care. Having an erratic schedule, like you would find in some commercial businesses of this size, works against that. To attract volunteers, consistent, predictable scheduling is important.

This operation is open 364 days per year. Shifts and volunteers are staffed to accommodate no shows.

Be Successful

This organization is well known in the community and in the region, and it means something to people to be able to say that they volunteer for Food Gatherers.

The Board of Directors is populated by people from some of the major corporations in the area, along with the U of Michigan. There is a social media presence, and ongoing media efforts to communicate the mission within the community

All of this makes it easy to recruit new volunteers.

There are also some recognition events, and team building activities that raise the value of the volunteer experience in the eyes of the participants.

Food Gatherers also participates in some of the local workforce training activities and has programs such as

"Healthy Pantry" nutritional advice and resources, along with job training.

Lessons from Volunteering: What to make of all of this?

This is a successful non-profit, that is well regarded in the community, and has survived for 35 years to perform a valued service. They are doing their jobs.

If success is measured in survival, consider that a for-profit business is only 20% likely to survive past their fifth year.

This organization is able to recruit and retain a workforce without paying them by treating people respectfully, having an organized operation with clear work instructions, and involving people in a higher mission.

The Four Root Causes Revisited

Let's go back and review this from the point of view of the Ishikawa method:

Human: Volunteers are engaged in the mission and will work without pay. Staffers are typically committed to the mission as well. Some may trade salary for job satisfaction.

Procedure: Processes are well thought out and organized, workers are treated to an efficient operation. The organization's supply chain, including sources of foods and local charities that do distribution are well established.

Resources: Well-established, modern infrastructure, able to provide the service with high levels of customer satisfaction

Controls: Engaged board members, transparent accounting systems. The organization understands its value in the community.

The Four Root Causes work in reverse. Attention to these four areas can lead to people doing their jobs and a rewarding work experience. Are there imperfections? No doubt, as there always are when dealing with people. There are your lessons.

Links and References

21 Lessons from Fast Food

We're going to address the important topic of Fast Food now.

I have picked on these places from time to time but can tell you that the fast-food industry is a modern miracle. I can attest that the Whopper in Chinatown in Kuala Lumpur tastes exactly like the Whopper down the road from me, and to that I say thank goodness because any time I ever had one over there I needed something familiar.

If you respect systems and process controls, you appreciate that for what it is, global standardization.

That's not to say that it is good for you, of course. I am not a nutritionist yet.

https://youtu.be/D3OpbHG9_ZI

Lessons from Fast Food

Why People Don't Do Their Jobs

The ACSI

According to the American Customer Fast Food index, here are the most highly rated brands in fast food. These are rated based on such factors as service accuracy, service speed, menu variety, functionality of the mobile app, and restaurant appearance.

Chick Fil A has been dominant in the last few years on this, although this year it has an inexplicable challenger.

We will now probe into this and try to figure out why this consistently happens.

Fast Food Restaurants

Company	2022	2023	% Change
Fast Food Restaurants	76	78	3%
Chick-fil-A	83	85	2%
Jimmy John's (Inspire Brands)	79	84	6%
All Others	79	82	4%
KFC (Yum! Brands)	78	81	4%
Papa Johns	76	80	5%

Here's the bottom four.

Jack in the Box	72	73	1%
Sonic (Inspire Brands)	74	72	-3%
Taco Bell (Yum! Brands)	72	71	-1%
McDonald's	68	69	1%

Chick Fil A History

Truett Cathy founded a restaurant, the Dwarf Grill, in 1946, in Hapeville GA. He opened the first Chick Fil A in the Greenbriar Mall in 1967.

Cathy was a pioneer in the "mall" food court franchise idea. He was one of the first people that recognized the potential, and based on this original idea, set forth the business systems that long ago became an essential element of the shopping mall experience.

Cathy's first free-standing Chick Fil A was opened in 1986, based on the same model, and has since grown to 2600 locations.

At this point, the company is selling more chicken in the world than KFC, despite having a third the number of locations, and being closed on Sunday.

People

The Chick Fil A hiring strategy is selectivity. They pick from a group of employees that some people will call "wholesome." In the last couple of years, some body art has snuck into the system, but that was once one of the things you never saw from the counter people.

The current average salary for a counter assistant at a Chick Fil A in Atlanta is $14.97. If you have been keeping track this is roughly the same as an airline baggage handler or a parking lot attendant, but higher than a starting teacher.

Counter Assistant hourly salaries in Atlanta, GA at Chick-fil-A

Job Title		Location
Counter Assistant	⌄	Atlanta

Average salary ❓

$14.97 per hour ⌄

↑ 9%   Above national average

Does this salary seem accurate?   Yes | No

Salary estimated from 1 employee, user, and past and present job advertisement on Indeed in the past 12 months.

Average Salaries at McDonald's

Popular Roles

Cashier	Shift Manager	Maintenance Person
$11.74 per hour	$15.50 per hour	$15.92 per hour
64 salaries reported	44 salaries reported	21 salaries reported

This compares to about $3 less for the comparable job for Mickey D's.

There is a comparison of employee satisfaction between Chick Fil A and McDonalds, on a website called "Comparably", and in this survey, 75% of Chick Fil A employees would recommend it to a friend, and employee retention is rated a "C", where at Mickey's, the employee recommendation rate is 67% and employee retention is rated "D+" which I guess means that the McDonald's employees are saying "Yeah, go ahead and work there but I already quit."

So, let's say that magically, the higher pay and chipper employees make for a happier workforce, which does a better job for its customers.

The investment in training the new employees varies from store to store. The McDonald's reference on this says, "they show me a video and send me to work," but in the Chick Fil A reference, they are a bit more thoughtful.

In the world of today, where low wage employees are in a bit of a shortage, the pre-Covid attitude toward this has not yet been restored.

Management
According to a 2019 article, it is easier to get into Harvard, as a percentage of the people who apply, than it is to become a Chick Fil A "Operator."

There is an extensive interview process, background checking, financial disclosure and a lot of other scrutiny that a prospective management undergoes. There will be more about that in a minute.

Processes
Like all franchise situations, both Chick Fil A and McDonalds have very detailed franchise agreements by which you agree to buy your signage, supplies, and other materials from the company.

That, of course, is the source of the famous meme of the McDonalds ice cream machines constantly being down, because the owners are required to buy spare parts from the main franchise HQ.

I have linked the franchise agreements for both Chick Fil A and McDonalds in the Links and References.

The interesting thing here is the selection of store locations. There is rather conflicting information among the sources on this topic, and I think it stems from the difference between the "average" customer vs. the Target customer.

Both companies see their main market as Gen X people, aged 45-55 at this time, but Chick Fil A is targeting a higher income customer. They are focused on suburban families with income in the $125K range that are frequent fast-food users.

McDonalds, according to some references, has a target market of somewhere in the $46-$60K range. So, it is true to say that the Chick Fil A is after a bit wealthier customer base.

How do they hope to manage that? I believe it is where they choose to locate their stores. If you put your stores in affluent neighborhoods, that's what your customers are going to be.

One of the criticisms in this is that there is an underlying racial bias in this, and I will let you divine that out of the data if you want. But having more affluent customers is a better business model.

I challenge some bright person working on his or her PhD dissertation on social justice to go through the Atlanta metro Chick Fil A and McDonald's locations and calculate the average income by zip code based on the address.

Resources

If there is a Chick Fil A in your area, I challenge you to go into the rest room, ref: McCaig's Law. Chick Fil A restrooms are very pleasant, overall. I go into a lot of public restrooms, as you know, so I am authoritative. Very often, at Chick Fil A they are fragrant, and have fresh flowers. The stores are newer, overall, so that may be part of the difference. Nice restrooms are a commitment.

McDonalds? Feel free to randomly sample a few McDonalds restrooms as well and compare. Part of it is that McDonald's customers may conceivably be less respectful and tend to trash the place more. That also comes with the territory of targeting a lower wage demographic.

Controls

If you get far enough into the franchise agreements, there is a section about controls.

In the case of Chick Fil A, you agree, as a condition of your franchise agreement, to allow your store to be "audited" on 72 hours' notice, at any time, for conformity to their standard operating procedures. This includes their methods, equipment, menu items and everything else that makes their branding consistent.

McDonald's auditors don't require 72 hours' notice. Those franchisees can be audited at any time during normal business hours for conformity. The McDonald's franchise agreement reads a lot like the ISO standard, which has ongoing internal audits, a document control procedure, and required procedures for a lot of other activities related to food safety and HACCP.

For your pleasure, I have linked some information on what the average income is for a McDonald's owner vs. a Chick Fil A Owner Operator, and I am not ready to say based on the references that the two are that much different.

There are a couple of other things.
McDonalds, being a publicly traded outfit like it is, is required to disclose financial information, including same store sales, growth rates, if any, and all the other data that are required by the SEC.

For the moment, the Chick Fil A corporation is privately held, and so they do not have to disclose all of that.

But they are also not constrained by the same financing rules and need for growth and can concentrate on operating the business they want; with the customers they want. Therein lies a bit of a problem, sometimes.

Chick Fil A Lawsuits and Other Difficulties
Most of the Chick Fil A restaurants are still located in the Southeast US, where there is still a lot of racial and religious tension.

A contributing factor is the open infusion of Christian religious activities among the staff and management. It's not a "requirement" that the employees adhere to this, but reportedly there is a "culture" of it.

Most recently, they had to pay a $4.4M Settlement because they were sued over delivery fees. During Covid, they had competitively low delivery fees, but increased the price of the food to compensate. Angry customers filed a class action suit.

They were sued in January of 2023 for Video Privacy violations by sharing data with Facebook as to who was watching one of its cute cartoons.

In 2020, they teamed up with Target to sue some chicken producers about price fixing.

In 2023 they were sued by a woman in Florida for selling her a "black" chicken nugget, which the woman ate, causing her foodborne illness.

In 2012 the company received a complaint on potential violation of the Employment Non-Discriminatory Act, for treatment of an LGBTQ employee and generous donations to an Anti- LGBTQ organization of some kind. There were several other lawsuits of this nature that happened at about the same time.

There have been multiple lawsuits throughout the years for discrimination against race and gender.

In 2002 they were sued for Muslim discrimination.

Chick Fil A has a stated policy of non-discrimination that states that they want "inclusiveness" and have hired a manager of non-discrimination. What they don't say is whether they still have a policy of "wholesomeness" as defined above when they hire the chipper counter workers that say, "my pleasure."

McDonalds Lawsuits

McDonalds has enough lawsuits that it warrants a Wikipedia page of its own for just the lawsuits. The classic one, of course, was the famous hot coffee spillage that ended up dooming most of society to lukewarm coffee for a generation.

McDonalds gets sued occasionally for discrimination as well. There is a lot of that going around.

What to Make of All of This: Lessons from Fast Food

I am ready to say based on the press releases and nationwide expansion that Chick Fil A's management is doing their jobs.

They produce a product that the customers like. They are also wisely choosing "wholesome" employees and "affluent" customers.

Their restrooms are nice, often with fresh flowers. Their customer service people deliver your meal to you with a pleasant smile.

Do they have some headwinds before they try to take over the world? I would say so, but it comes with the territory.

Links and References

22 The Coach Who Did His Job

This is the story of the coach who did his job.

A coach, in the sports sense, has three jobs. One is to train and be a positive influence on the life of the person that he or she is coaching. Another is to be a positive influence and contribute to the sport. The third one is to win. In this era, coaching success is identified closely with winning.

A fourth one, or maybe a constraint that regulates the other three, is to not cheat.

A coach can have a long, successful career doing two of the three things above.

So, this is the story of the Coach Who Did His Job. His name was Berny Wagner.

Background Information

The high jump is a track and field event, field event specifically. The contest is to see who can jump over a bar that is elevated above the ground. The competitors take turns trying to jump over the bar. The bar is incrementally raised, until they start to miss. The competitor at the end, having jumped the height that no one else was able to, is the winner.

https://youtu.be/wQi-nPVoMhc

This event requires something called "kinesthetic awareness." The competitor runs toward the bar at full speed, and then transfers his or her horizontal momentum to vertical. It requires speed and timing to do this optimally.

The accepted method for the high jump prior to 1950 was called the "Western Roll." The competitor ran toward the bar, jumped vertically, and rolled over with the bar facing his or her belly button. It was replaced for a few years by the "Straddle technique" which is illustrated here:

By "accepted method" I mean the "standard operating procedure." Competitors and coaches in this event subscribed to this as the best method for doing this event and taught young athletes this method.

Dick Fosbury (1947-2023)

Dick Fosbury, born in Portland in 1947, was an exceptionally gifted athlete who was a high jumper.

He was incompetent as a high jumper at age 16 at Medford, Oregon, high school because he could not master the complexity of either of the other techniques.

He invented or otherwise experimented with a new technique, namely going over the bar backward. Within a year or two, this fellow had perfected the method to the extent needed to be successful.

Side topic is that at this time, the landing material in the US was changed from sawdust to foam rubber. That allowed the athlete to land on his or her head occasionally without consequences.

By 1965, he was state runner up in Oregon for high school competitors, jumping 6 feet 5 inches which is still impressive for a high school high jumper today

Berny Wagner

Berny Wagner had served in the US Navy in the Pacific during World War II and graduated with a master's degree from Stanford in 1948.

He began coaching in high schools throughout northern California and Oregon and became head track and cross-country coach at Oregon State University in 1965, at the same time Fosbury was graduating from high school.

295

He could recognize Fosbury's athletic gifts, but wouldn't let him use his method, the Fosbury Flop, in the varsity meets, confining him to the Western Roll, except for Freshman meets.

When he cleared 6 ft. 10 inches in one of those meets, he said "That's it. No more plan A, we're going to Plan B."

Wagner studied the technique, to understand the merits, and then tried to teach the same technique to the younger jumpers.

By 1968, Fosbury was the national NCAA champion, won the US Olympic trials, and then ended up winning the gold medal in the 1968 Olympics in Tokyo.

Here is a quote from Marcel Hetu:

"Start with the three C's -- caring, concerned and compassionate," says Marcel Hetu, who ran for Wagner at College of San Mateo in 1964 and '65. " 'Berny' was coach, mentor, father figure -- all those things for so many

296

of us trying to find ourselves academically, athletically and personally."

"Berny changed my life," says John Radetich, among the fleet of 7-foot-high jumpers Wagner had at Oregon State. "I met my wife at Corvallis. I competed for the greatest high jump school of all- time. I got my degree. He was responsible for all of that. I'm forever indebted."

"To say Berny had an everlasting effect on thousands upon thousands would be an understatement," says Kelly Sullivan, head coach of OSU's current women's program. "He truly was an exceptional individual, one who comes around once in a lifetime."

"He knew every event and every scientific approach to that event," says Hetu, who was California community college mile champion in 1965. "From a psychological standpoint, he understood how to prepare his athlete for a race, even after the race. He worked on the psychological, technical and physical sides of preparing you. He was a holistic coach. He understood all the facets."

Adaptability

The interesting thing about this story is that this is exactly the kind of fellow, ex-military who usually doesn't want to accept change. The more common approach was to say "my way or the highway."

But he used data, and changed the procedure in a controlled manner, in which he understood the nuances of the method. That is why he was able to transfer this improved technique to other athletes. During his career, Wagner coached 7 athletes who jumped over 7 feet, which is still considered an impressive achievement.

The current world record is 8 feet ¼ inch, set in 1993, is the longest standing record in the history of the event. It was set by Javier Sotomayor from Cuba, and this was during the period when another technical innovation, use of steroids, was prevalent.

I have placed a link to this effect.

Change Resistance and the Law of Diffusion

According to the references, this method of high jumping was not embraced by everybody immediately, despite its obvious success. This is, of course, one of the definitions of Entrenched Mediocrity.

I can attest to this personally. It was still not the prevailing method of high jump technique in Iowa in the late 1970's.

This is a phenomenon that is called the "law of diffusion." Here is how it works.

There are innovators, and early adopters, that very often face some societal resistance to any kind of innovation. At a certain point, the innovation becomes "mainstream." The mainstream, plus the early adopters, make up about ⅔ of society. The remaining population consists of slow adopters and then there is a certain fraction of the population, about 15%, which refuses to change. These are the people that today, refuse to use cell phones, and are still doing what they do.

I guess that also says a lot about that part of Iowa.

According to the article by LaFrance, the key moment in the innovation is the communication between the early adopters and the first of the mainstream. Fosbury, and Wagner of course, invested time to understand the innovation, and then were able to successfully

298

communicate the benefits to the mainstream. This idea was pioneered by Rogers in 1962 and is a marketing concept.

Law of Diffusion of Innovations
(Rogers, 1962)

The Brill Bend

If you are Canadian, you may wish to think about Debbie Brill, who pioneered the use of this method as a 13-year-old at roughly the same time.

She was competing internationally at the age of 15 and became the first North American female to clear 6 feet. She also held the women's indoor world record, and won two gold medals at the Commonwealth Games, over a 12-year period.

She was ranked number one in the world in 1980 but was deprived of her chance to compete for an Olympic Medal because of the cancellation of the games that year which were to be held in Moscow, due to the USSR invasion of Afghanistan.

299

Debbie's coach was Lionel Pugh, from the U of British Columbia, who also did his job. He produced multiple Canadian national champions, and more than half of the current records from this school were made during his coaching tenure, which was back in the 1970's and early 1980's.

The Coach who Did His Job

So here, in the form of Berny Wagner, is the coach that did his job. He helped several enormously gifted athletes, helped develop an innovative standard
operating procedure, took advantage of changes in the infrastructure (Foam Rubber) and understood the control methods, and became immortal, among those who are interested in the High Jump.

He is not a household name among the non-high-jumpers I suppose.

He did this by not adhering to the standard operating procedure, but by changing in a controlled manner. He also figured out how to navigate the Diffusion Effect, which may have been his main achievement.

There is hope for humanity.

Links and References

Why People Don't Do Their Jobs

23 Final Exam

Here, in the spirit of Berny Wagner, is a little exam that might be fun for you, the reader, as you draw to the close of this. This sort of exam is common in business school, so think of it that way. You've been given a priceless education on the topic of how some of the management theory doesn't work.

Tim limit is one hour and fifteen minutes, which is the length of time it took for me to get my food the other night

Case 1: Suburban Restaurant

The venue was an independently owned restaurant/drinking establishment in a suburban strip shop. The clientele during the week is middle aged, but there is sometimes a bit different type of "night life" on the weekends

It was Tuesday night. The place hosts a trivia contest and there is extra space for birthday parties, and this particular night there were two.

I was with a group of people at the time.

https://youtu.be/44U9XqNYwPY

The Hostess
We entered the place and were greeted by the hostess, a young female who looked up from her social media. She was wholesome, and non-threatening. After a brief interaction, we were seated in a booth in a corner of the place.

The Server
The server was young, male, and had a significant investment in body art. He didn't look particularly wholesome. He took our orders and disappeared into the back.

There was a buzz in the place, as there often is. There are a lot of TVs and some Keno and this is a popular place if there is some sort of sporting event. The restaurant itself was not especially crowded. There were empty tables, but there was a lot of non-specific noise in the room, in addition to the trivia.

About 20 minutes went by.

One of the food runners came out with a Taco Salad and asked if any of us had ordered it. We said "nah.' A few minutes later, another food runner came out with some orphan calamari. Within a few more minutes, the server himself returned, flipped through a ratty notebook with our orders on it, and re-took our orders.

The server mumbled something to the effect that someone had re-numbered the tables, and the runners didn't know where their food was going. That didn't really explain why our order hadn't started after 20 minutes.

We did notice one thing, though, which was that the server was assigned to an entire section of the restaurant, a dozen tables and booths or so, to cover by himself.

About 30 minutes later the food arrived. At least it was warm and seemed like it was freshly cooked. This was mainly bar food, some combination of burgers and salads like you would get in suburbia.

The Manager
Nada. Nobody around there looked like a manager, to the extent that a manager looks a certain way.

The Problem Statement
Late food. It took over an hour to be served bar food. There was apparent bafflement on the part of the staff that

caused us and a lot of people not to get their food on time. We could tell we weren't the only ones.

There is no telling how the birthday party was going from a service standpoint.

Other Information
Was there any feedback loop, or data gathering that alerted the management to a problem? That is not particularly known. This spot does not use the new point-of-sale equipment yet, with the tablets and styluses and electronic data gathering.

We also didn't venture back into the kitchen, like Gordon Ramsey would have done in this situation. It's sort of a pity, we might have learned a lot. As it is, we know enough.

The restrooms are a bit rough, which is sort of a theme of the place. It is intended not to be too nice as part of their casual dining branding.

The checks were delivered incident-free. The waiter correctly billed us and got the right check for the right party.

Questions:
Which of the following statements are likely to be made by the Hostess? (More than one may apply)

I just love my job. The work is easy, and they don't mind if I surf social media in my spare time.

I hate my job, I have to be on my feet the whole time, and the manager complains if I surf social media in working hours.

The manager goes home at 6. I've never actually met the owner.

This job is fine until I start to build my following as an influencer.

Which of the following statements are likely to be made by the Server?

I hate trivia night. It's a big crowd and nobody drinks. I can't turn the tables over fast enough.

Who the hell changed the table numbering system and didn't tell me? The runners are delivering the food to the wrong tables, and it makes me look like a chump.

Where the hell is Millicent, my co-worker. This is the third time this month she skipped work. I guess she has childcare issues but that is not really my problem. I have to cover the dining room.

Who the hell scheduled two birthday parties on trivia night?

I love my job. I want it to be my career forever.

Six years of college down the drain.

Which of the following statements are likely to be made by the Runners?

Nobody told me where to deliver this stuff.

This is my first week, and I feel like quitting already.

At least I get a free shot of Fireball occasionally

I've wanted to be a food runner in an annoying restaurant since I was 3.

Which of the following statements are likely to be made by the Manager?

This is a smooth operation, and everything is wonderful.

Problems? What problems? Nobody told me about any problems.

My old job had a better point-of-sale system. We can't track anything here, especially wait times.

I hate this job. If I hadn't slept through math class, I might have been successful.

I hate this job, but it is better than working in a factory.

I just can't find enough good people nowadays.

All the boss does is give me hell, and I never even see her. She shows up once a week and I have to lie and tell her that everything is fine in here. All she worries about is sales dollars.

I like my boss. She is very supportive, and if I need more people, she is happy to approve the hire.

Who the hell scheduled two birthday parties on Trivia night? My poor cook and runners are going to be swamped.

Which of the following statements is likely to be made by the owner?

I never ran a place like this before. I am pleased at how it is going.

I've never really been in there at night. I wonder what kind of crowd I am drawing?

I have a lot of trouble keeping good help. The Amazon place is opening a few miles away. Maybe I will get a few more customers.

The cops were called to this place last Saturday. I wonder why?

I have a firm grasp on all of the processes and systems in the place, and I am always trying to improve my customer experience.

I like the workers for the most part. I never hear any complaints.

Essay Questions:

You are the celebrity rescuer that oversees trying to fix this place.

The owner may not know that he or she has a problem, since there is no system for customer feedback. She doesn't think it needs to be fixed.

The manager and a few of the more alert crew would probably prefer not to get another job, but they are not emotionally attached to the place.

Using the four root causes of everything, design a plan to improve the customer experience in this place, which, for the moment, already has plenty of customers.

What sort of problems do you expect in changing the culture, because the place appears to already have plenty of customers (for now)?

What do you think is the likely strategic direction of the organization? Does it matter if you don't have one?

Who would you fire first? Who would you promote first? If you don't have any lower-level employees with promotion potential, what does that say about your hiring and employee retention? What infrastructure improvements are needed?

What is potentially bad about the Amazon place opening up down the street? What is your plan for dealing with it?

What is potentially bad about the fact that 100% of your customers need to drive to get to the place?

Discuss how these principles can be used to troubleshoot and potentially improve any type of organization, especially in manufacturing.

Remember, you have an hour and fifteen minutes.

Copying from your neighbor will be futile.

Case 2: This Thing

This thing is one of those machines that one uses to put air in car tires. This particular one is next to a Wal-Mart gas station.

The way it is supposed to work is that when someone needs air, they drive up, swipe their credit card, and the device turns on either a compressor or a vacuum cleaner, and the machine turns on for a few minutes while you put air into your tires or use the vacuum.

This one has been destroyed somehow. The part of the gadget that reads the credit card has been knocked out, probably because someone wanted to get at the quarters that supposedly are in it. The hose itself looks like it has been run over a few times.

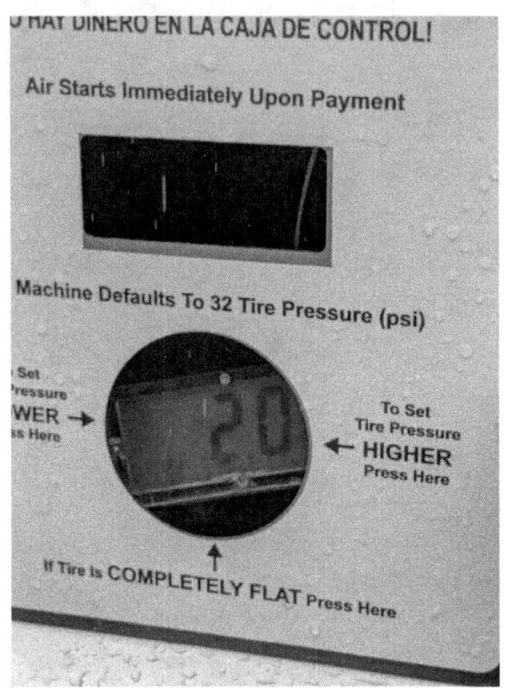

Problem Statement

The Air Machine is trashed and inoperable.

At a minimum, there is customer pain because this thing is in pieces, and it is ugly. It's a message to the universe on the part of the organization that they really don't care whether your tire is low on air or not. They're happy to send you onto the road with a potential danger situation. Maybe they don't see that as their responsibility.

Or they really don't care whether their gas stations are ugly.

Or it doesn't bother them that they lost at least $5 in revenue because neither I nor the person behind me was able to put air in their tires.

Additional Context

The identifying sticker is for something called "CSC Serviceworks." Here is a web link:

CSC Serviceworks Website

https://www.cscsw.com/services/air-service/

It looks like you can buy one of these machines for about $6500, if you choose to have one of these set up somewhere.

It is not at all clear who, if anyone, takes the money out of them, and empties out the contents of the vacuum cleaner, or, for that matter, who replaces the hoses and does maintenance on them, or for that matter, who even owns it.

Questions:

Who do you complain to? Which, if any, of these employees can or would fix it, or give you a refund in the unfortunate event that you were able to get it to read your credit card but not turn on (Select one or more.)

The gas station attendant (locked in the little building.)

The Wal Mart store manager?

Some 800 number on the machine?

What is the fundamental business problem with this device?

It costs $6500 to install one of these things and about fifteen minutes for some drunk to destroy it at midnight

It requires cooperation on the part of some human to service it and feed information back to you, the owner of the machine, whomever you may be.

This is a sure-fire money maker and everyone should have one or more of these as a side hustle.

In light of McCaig's Law, estimate the probability that many of these machines all over the region are equally screwed up. _____

In a general way, from the point of view of CSCSW, what's the probability that CSC has already gone bankrupt because they couldn't find a labor force reliable enough to service these machines? _____

Why, **if you are the Wal Mart corporation**, would you bother with this type of thing in the first place? What were you thinking?

Case 3: Entrenched Mediocrity
In either or both of the above examples, there is a management system breakdown. Considering the several definitions of Entrenched Mediocrity, discuss what, if anything, can or should be done about any of this.

There are the four working definitions of "Entrenched Mediocrity."

An obvious beneficial change is resisted, especially for non-technical reasons

The organization accepts mediocrity to avoid the cost of change

A widely known problem is allowed to continue despite obvious risk

Overhead activities become more important than production

Customers are not satisfied, nothing changes, no one gets fired. As a society, what are the options?

Links and References

About the Author

Here is a little Bio information

I am a working quality auditor with more than 500 audits and have worked in some of the global brand name companies, as the most customer-facing member of an international quality system organization.

My background story is in formulation development in Rubber and Tires, and I am co-contributor for three US patents. After graduating from that, I used my quality systems and business analysis authority to be a contributing writer with over 1 million page views on a famous internet financial analysis website.

I also have more than 170,000 views on my YouTube site and have been a favorite trainer on the topic of internal auditing, and the ISO9001 standard.

On my website, www.Jimshell.com, you'll find a project list, a resume and a lot of blog posts and other content that you will find entertaining and informative.